1001
Ways NOT to be Romantic

Joe Magadatz

Casanova Press
New York

Bookstore distribution: Login Publishers Consortium
800-626-4330

Giftstore distribution: Sourcebooks
800-798-2475

"The great question
that has never been answered
and which I have not yet been able to answer,
despite my thirty years of research into the
feminine soul, is:
What does woman want?"

~ Sigmund Freud

"Who *cares*?!"

~ Joe Magadatz

Copyright © 1993 by Joe Magadatz & Casanova Press

All rights reserved.
(You make-a the copies, we break-a you legs. *Kapish*?)

First printing.
Printed in the good old US of A.
10 9 8 7 6 5 4 3 2 1 — *Blast off!*

Published by
Casanova Press
P.O. Box 313
Naperville, IL 60566

Cover illustration by M.L.B.

Publisher's Cataloging in Publication Data

Magadatz, Joe, 19??
1001 Ways *Not* To Be Romantic

Includes index.
1. Humor. 2. Relationships. I. Title.

Library of Congress Catalog Card Number
00-00000000000-0000000-000000

ISBN 1-883518-27-X

Dedications

To the millions of men and women who feel pressured by the self righteous Self-Helpers and the Politically Correct busybodies of the world.

And, of course, to my ex-wives. . .
F.U.B.A.R.

✦ Table of Contents ✦

- Aaaaaaauuugh! 1
- Absolut Fun .... π
- Actions Speak Louder Than Words 4
- Aggravation 5
- America, America 6
- Babies & Other Mistakes 8
- Bad First Dates 9
- Bad Habits 10
- Battle of the Sexes 11
- Beam Me Up, Scotty 12
- Behind the Eight Ball 13
- Bonnie & Clyde 14
- Born Losers 16
- Boston Baked Beans 17
- Bowling For Dollars 18
- Boys Will Be Boys 19
- Brides & Other Insane People 20
- Burp! 21
- But Seriously, Folks 23
- Cheapskates Unite! 25
- Co-Dependency for Fun & Profit 25
- Dangerous Liaisons 27
- Dear Mr. Unromantic 28
- Deep Freeze 30
- Deep Throat 31
- Diamonds Are a Girl's Best Friend 33
- Divorce: The Ultimate Cure 35
- Doctor Demento 36
- Doctor Doolittle 37
- Doctor Seuss 38
- Doctor Strangelove 39
- Doomed From the Start 40
- Doozies 42
- Eggheads 44
- Excuuuse Me! 45
- Familiarity Breeds Contempt 46
- Fatal Attraction 47
- Faux Pas 48
- For Marrieds Only 49
- For Men Only 51
- For Women Only 52
- Funny Business 54
- Gal Stuff 55
- Games People Play 55
- Garter Belts Galore! 57
- Go Ahead, Make My Day! 59
- Going Bonkers 60
- Golf & Other Unromantic Stuff 62
- Gone With the Wind 63
- Good Grief! 64
- Guy Stuff 65
- Gym Class 66
- Happiness Is a Warm Gun 67
- Happy Anniversary 68
- Ho-Ho-Ho! 70
- Home Alone 71
- Homer Simpson, Revisited 72
- Honey, I Blew Up the Relationship 73
- Honeymoon Hell 76
- Hooters! 76
- How To Ruin Your Life 77
- I Was Just Thinking 80
- I'm Dysfunctional, You're Dysfunctional 81
- If God Had Meant Man to be Romantic 82
- Immaturity & Other Techniques 83
- In-Laws & Other Household Pests 84

✦ Table of Contents ✦

- ☆ Inappropriate Gestures 85
- ☆ Inappropriate Gifts 86
- ☆ Isn't That Special?! 89
- ☆ It's a Mad, Mad, Mad, Mad World 91
- ☆ It's All in Your Mind 93
- ▼ Jerks R Us 94
- ➣ Lessons from Nerds 96
- ➣ Lessons from the Bible 98
- ➣ Lessons from The 3 Stooges 99
- ➣ Life Is a Cabaret 100
- ➣ Losers & Weiners 101
- ➣ Love Is A Many Splintered Thing 103
- ➣ Love Is Blind 104
- ✓ Male Bashing 104
- ✓ Mama Mia! 106
- ✓ Men vs. Women 107
- ✓ Mindset of an Unromantic 108
- ✓ Miscommunicating for Fun & Profit 109
- ✓ Money Can't Buy You Love .. 111
- ✓ Monotony— Not Monogamy 112
- ✓ More Bad Habits 113
- ✓ Most Illogical 114
- ✓ Movie Madness 115
- ✓ Music & Other Mush 117
- ✓ Mutant Teenage Ninja Turtles 119
- ○ Nagging & Other Techniques 120
- ○ Nice Guys Finish Last 122
- ○ *Norm!!* 124
- ▼ Oh, Shit! 124
- ✻ Playboy of the Western World 38
- ❥ Real Men Aren't Romantic .. 127
- ❥ Real *Women* Aren't Romantic 128
- ❥ Reality 101 130
- ❥ Revenge Is Sweet 132
- ❥ Run Like Hell 133
- ✻ Science Fiction 135
- ✻ Setting the Record Straight . 136
- ✻ Sex, Sex, Sex 137
- ✻ Sports, Sports, Sports 140
- ✻ Surprise! 142
- ✦ The Beer Barrel Polka 144
- ✦ The Far Side 145
- ✦ The Gospel According to Joe 147
- ✦ The Heartbreak of VD 149
- ✦ The Way We Were 150
- ✦ The World According to Joe 151
- ✦ Travel Tips 152
- ✦ Truly Tasteless 154
- ❑ Unromantic Classics 155
- ❑ Unromantic Ideas 156
- ■ Virtual Reality 157
- ✢ Wedding Bell Blues 158
- ✢ Weird & Wacky 159
- ✢ What Do Women Want? 161
- ✢ What's Your Sign? 162
- ✢ Wheel of Fortune 163
- ✢ Where's the Beef? 164
- ✢ Where's Waldo? 165
- ✢ Who Asked You? 166
- ✢ Why Bother? 167
- ✢ Wilted Flowers 168
- ✢ Women's Lib 169
- ☞ X-Rated 170
- ✹ Your Profession: Romantic or Unromantic? 172
- ☛ Zzzzzzz 176
- ❥ Unromantic Coupons 178

Acknowledgments

T.B.
B. McH.
C. McG.
National Association of Toaster Manufacturers
H.L. Mencken
J.(n) G.
A.P.
PDQ Bach

About the Author

Joe Magadatz is, perhaps, the most unromantic man in America. Granted, his reputation isn't as big as Rush Limbaugh's—but then again, neither is his ego.

Joe is a veteran of the Battle of the Sexes. He is currently back in the Singles Infantry, having been wounded twice in the Matrimonial Skirmishes.

Joe was born in Pittsburgh, raised in L.A., and educated in Memphis. Joe has traveled the length and breadth of this country in search of love (well, sex)—he was married in New York, divorced in Muncie, married again in Las Vegas, and divorced again in Miami.

Joe's sophomoric humor and sarcastic wit earn him scathing looks from his friends' wives on a regular basis. This, combined with the fact that he can type, are his qualifications for writing this book. (Hey, if Dave Barry can do it . . .)

Publisher's Note

All of the products mentioned in this book are real, as are the companies, phone numbers and addresses. (Just because things sound weird or outlandish doesn't necessarily mean they aren't true.) As for the rest of the material in the book, if it sounds *implausible*, it's probably true; and if it sounds *improbable*, it's probably a product of Joe Magadatz's over-active imagination. We make no claim as to what's true, what's stretched, and what's a pack of lies. All we know is that we laughed our collective asses off when we read this book!

If you find any errors or typos in this book, please don't send them to us. We don't care. You may, however, want to circle the errors and show them to your friends in a feeble attempt to demonstrate your mental acuity and intelligence. Your friends, however, will note that no truly intelligent person would be reading this book in the first place; and in the *second* place, they will take your behavior as further proof of your anal-retentive nature.

Joe takes great liberties with the English language. He says he takes "Artistic License"—but we suspect it's simply lack of knowledge of proper grammar.

Introduction

I believe that you can make *anything* unromantic, if you'll only use a little creativity. It is my hope to inspire you to get in touch with your true, if uncouth, nature—and express it proudly!

I also believe that society is harmed by bone-headed romantic notions. We too often make decisions based on *emotions*, and not *facts*. I'm trying to bring a little perspective to our lives. In fact, this book is a much-needed public service!

Many people have asked (... well, my *Mom* asked) how this book was conceived and written. I was sitting around the local pub with my buddy Michael Kropenjaic, discussing the nature of the universe and ogling pretty girls, when the topic turned to Why Love Turns Us Into Idiots. I started jotting notes down on napkins. [Picture Norm and Cliff sitting around *Cheers*, and you've got the picture.] [And no, I don't have "Norm's good looks and Cliff's clever wit" as more than one person has suggested. *Geez!*] Anyway, after about two years of hanging out at the pub, and more than our fair share of hangovers, I had this pile of napkins that my friends said I should turn into a book. Well, after many misadventures—including a dinner party at which my second wife accidentally set the table with my book-napkins, causing two ladies to faint and one guy to laugh so hard that he snorted wine out of his nose (needless to say, this ruined the dinner party—but it helped launch my literary career)—a foolish publisher took on the project, and, well, here we are!

My hope is that this book will help people in some small way—by cutting through the bullshit of the self-help books that are flooding the bookstores. I hope to capitalize on the natural tension that exists between the sexes, and exploit it for fun and profit.

This book was written primarily from a male point-of-view. I do want to acknowledge, however, that there are some World Class unromantics who are women. Welcome to the Club, babes! As for the rest of you—Hey, find your *own* dates!

Reprinted with permission of Creators Syndicate, Inc., Wizard of Id © 1993

Aaaaaaauuugh!

1

Being unromantic is not merely a habit or an aberration—it's a *lifestyle*.

2-8

This book is predicated on the beliefs that...
- ☐ Sports are the Purpose of Life
- ☐ Love is a figment of Shakespeare's imagination.
- ☐ Sex is a figment of Freud's imagination.
- ☐ Nice guys finish last.
- ☐ Give a woman an inch and she'll take a mile.
- ☐ Give a man an inch and he'll claim it's *eight* inches.
- ☐ Roseanne Arnold is a nightmare I hope to wake up from soon.

9

Famous last words from former romantics:
- ✦ "I really don't think that having children will change our lifestyle."
- ✦ "He says the pre-nuptial agreement is merely a formality."
- ✦ "She says her mother's only going to live with us for a few months."
- ✦ "How much could a little mink coat cost?"

10

Literary Review of Allegedly Romantic Classics
Romeo and Juliet

Exciting sword fight. Then boy meets girl. Families disapprove. Boy woos girl from below balcony. A little hanky-panky. Plot twist obviously lifted from *Twin Peaks*, in which she takes poison, but it's only temporary; and she sends boy a message, which gets intercepted—anyway, things get all mixed-up. She "poisons" self; he, grief-stricken, stabs self; she awakens to discover him dead; she, of course, kills self. [Will somebody *please* explain to me why this is considered romantic?]

✦ *AAAAAAAUGH!* ✦

11

A sure-fire way to kill the romance in your life: Work together in business.

12-15

Dates from Hell:

→ He takes you to Championship Wrestling.
→ She takes you to a friend's wedding.
→ He takes you to meet his mother.
→ She takes you to a movie: *Fatal Attraction*.

16

One of the most unromantic vacations you could *possibly* take is a "Wagon Train" trip through the Olde West. (You can tell it's genuine when they spell "olde" with an "e" at the end!) One couple (that is no longer together) reported to me that a horse-drawn wagon traveling over dirt paths is "The most uncomfortable mode of transportation yet devised by man." Hemorrhoid suffers take note! For more ("Yee-hah!") info, call: Missouri: 800-877-1234. Kansas: 800-252-6727. Nebraska: 800-228-4307. Wyoming: 800-225-5996.

17

*"Romantic Love is mental illness.
But it's a pleasurable one. It's a drug. It distorts reality, and that's the point of it. It would be impossible to fall in love with someone that you really saw."*
~ Fran Lebowitz

18

Unromantics are not unromantic out of *spite* . . . We just have better things to do with our time.

✦ ABSOLUT FUN ✦

Absolut Fun

19

Make sure your travel plans include a stop at the Museum of Whiskey History in Bardstown, Kentucky! On display are stills, a Victorian bar, and antique bottles, jugs and barrels. Of special interest is an 1854 bottle produced by Philadelphia liquor dealer E.G. Booz—from whom the word "booze" originated. Boy, I'll bet his family is proud of *him*!

"DON'T WAIT UP... I'M GOING DOWN TO ARTHUR'S BAR TO WORK ON OUR RELATIONSHIP."

Reprinted with permission of King Features Syndicate, Inc., The Lockhorns © 1992

20

Take it from your Uncle Joe, most women can't tell the difference between *Dom Perignon* and *Boone's Farm*.

21

When your buddies are consoling you following another romantic disaster, they're likely to say a lot of things in "code." This list of common phrases will help you decipher what they're really saying to you:

- He says: "So, it's over, huh?"
- He means: "She finally dumped you like a hot potato!"
- He says: "She's not good enough for you, anyway."
- He means: "Oh, boy! Now *I've* got a shot at her!"
- He says: "Hey, our emotions make all of us do things we later regret."
- He means: "Love turns us into babbling idiots!"
- He says: "You two don't belong together, anyway."
- He means: "You look like Beavis, and she looks like Cindy Crawford."
- He says: "We guys gotta stick together!"
- He means: "Maybe he'll buy me a beer!"

Actions Speak Louder Than Words

22

One great way to be unromantic *and* remain above criticism is to take-on a Cause. It is well-known that members of extreme groups—such as Greenpeace, NOW, and the Republican Party—put their cause before *anything* else in their lives, including their relationships.

23

A good, smelly cigar can be a better romance deterrent than a *dozen* cloves of garlic.

24

"She was so glad to see me go, that I have almost a mind to come again, that she may again have the same pleasure."
~ Samuel Johnson

25

- Romantics celebrate the 12 Days of Christmas.
- Unromantics celebrate the 7 Days of Superbowl Week.

26

- Romantics take time to stop and smell the roses.
- Unromantics take time to shower only when they start to smell.

27

- Romantics know all the words to *As Time Goes By*.
- Unromantics know all the words to *The Brady Bunch* theme song.

28

- Romantics are enchanted by *Fantasy Island*.
- Unromantics are enchanted by *Gilligan's Island*.

Aggravation

29

- Romantics practice the guitar so they can accompany themselves as they sing lovesongs to their lovers.
- Unromantics practice the bagpipes so they can irritate everyone within a 3-mile radius.

30

"I hate women because they always know where things are."
~ James Thurber

31

Tape *Miss July* to the refrigerator door—as a way to inspire her to lose weight.

America, America

32

Through a highly scientific and very secret methodology I have identified *the most unromantic cities and towns in America*: [Please don't call to complain because your town isn't listed. The judge's decisions are *final*.]

Snead, Alabama
Juneau, Alaska
Skull Valley, Arizona
Grubbs, Arkansas
Weed Patch & Los Angeles, California
Swink, Colorado
Ellington, Connecticut
Smyrna, Delaware
Apopka & Miami, Florida
Lumpkin, Georgia
Fruitland, Idaho
[There is *nowhere* in Hawaii that isn't romantic.]
Naperville, Illinois
Gas City, Indiana
Mechanicsville, Iowa

✦ AMERICA, AMERICA ✦

Burden, Kansas
Bourbon, Kentucky
Cut Off, Louisiana
Portland, Maine
Whiskey Bottom, Maryland
Worcester, Massachusetts
Bad Axe & Muskegon, Michigan
Good Thunder, Minnesota
Yazoo City, Mississippi
Black Jack, Missouri
Flathead, Montana
Hooker, Nebraska
Pahrump & Las Vegas, Nevada
Little Boars Head, New Hampshire
Newark, New Jersey
Oil Center, New Mexico
New York City & East Rochester, New York
Winston-Salem & Fayetteville, North Carolina
[*Everyplace* in North Dakota is *equally* unromantic.]
Blue Ball & Cleveland, Ohio
Broken Arrow, Oklahoma
Crook, Oregon
Pittsburgh & DuBois, Pennsylvania
Providence, Rhode Island
Gluck, South Carolina
[Everyplace *except* Wakonda, South Dakota, is unromantic.]
Knoxville, Tennessee
Dallas & Waco, Texas
Salt Lake City, Utah
Putney, Vermont
Dumfries, Virginia
Twisp & Walla Walla, Washington
Neopit, Wisconsin
Lusk, Wyoming

Babies & Other Mistakes

33-35

- A sure-fire way to stamp-out the romance in your life: Have a baby.
- A sure-fire way to kill the romance in your life once and for all: Have a second child.
- A sure-fire way to tell when you've totally lost your mind: When you have six or more children.

36

I think that a big part of the reason why humanity is so messed-up is that we insist on combining three very different concepts: Love, Sex, and procreation. I think Mr. Spock had the right idea. You see, Vulcans effectively ignore the opposite sex for seven years. Then they go on a mating frenzy, where the sexual urge blots out all reason and logic. [Sounds like some of my fraternity brothers! Except they were on a beer-induced *four-year* frenzy.] Anyway—the Vulcans "do it," and then they're done with it for another seven years. Where do I sign-up?

37

Babies. Children. The pitter-patter of tiny feet. The cherubic faces . . . Projectile vomiting. Colic. Diapers. Midnight feedings. College funds. *Barney.* The End of Your Life as You Have Known It. {Thanks to B. Jones.}

Bad First Dates

38

For you gals: Take him to see the movie *Fatal Attraction*.

39

For you guys: Take her to see the movie *Nine 1/2 Weeks*.

40

For you guys: Take her to see the movie *Boxing Helena*. Here's the story: Insecure doctor amputates the arms and legs of his beloved so she can't leave him. Cute, huh?

41

A walk through the park is unromantic—if it's Central Park.

42

While on a date, drop by the office to make "Just one more call." Women *hate* this. {Thanks to A.P.}

43

While paying for dinner on a first date... pull a condom out of your wallet and say, "Just want you to know I'm always prepared!" Guaranteed to go over like a lead balloon.

44

Guys, forget your wallet on your first elegant dinner date.

Bad Habits

45

Golf.

46

Smoking. Cigarettes are truly unromantic. Many psychological and sociological studies have confirmed that foul breath, brown teeth and smelly clothes are romantic turn-offs.

47

But if you want to take your smoking habit a quantum leap forward (or backwards—depending on how you look at it)—take up *cigars*. A good El Producto or fine Cuban cigar will not only take years off your life, it will keep 99.9% of all women from approaching you.

48

It is truly bad form to serve white wine with steak, or red wine with fish. Unromantics have come up with the perfect answer to this dilemma. *Beer.* Beer goes with everything.

49

Bad Habit #504: Picking your nose.

50

Bad Habit #223: Scratching your crotch. (Bonus Points for scratching your butt. Super Bonus Points for doing either in public.)

Battle of the Sexes

51

"The war between the sexes is the only one in which both sides regularly sleep with the enemy."
~ Quentin Crisp

52-55

- ☞ Compare her cooking to your mother's.
- ☞ Compare her looks to your secretary's.
- ☞ Compare her lovemaking to that of the girl you last dated before you married her.
- ☞ Compare how she looks in a bathing suit to the Sports Illustrated swimsuit models.

56-59

(Turn-about is fair play, right? . . .)

- Compare his looks to Mel Gibson's.
- Compare his bank account to H. Ross Perot's.
- Compare his balding head to photos of him as a teenager.
- Compare the size of his penis to that of your last lover before you married him.

60-61

Some advice:

Ladies: Never let your man forget his faults. (He may *seem* to resent your nagging, but deep down he'll appreciate your concern.)

Men: When a woman says "No" she means "Yes."

Beam Me Up, Scotty

62

The Prize for The Person Who Has Done the Most to Take the Romance Out of Sex—for the fifth year in a row—goes to Madonna. Thanks, babe. Your book *Sex* was pointless yet tasteless, and your album *Erotica* was anything but. Keep up the good work.

63

"Isn't there *anything* good about romance?" you might ask. I've given this a lot of thought, and perhaps surprisingly, the answer is *yes*—there is *one* good thing about romance: It keeps the authors of self-help books gainfully employed. Otherwise, these know-it-all busybodies would be driven to haranguing us from street corners with their sappy philosophies, while begging us for quarters. I suppose it's better that they spend most of their time alone in their offices writing books, and the remainder of their time on TV talk shows.

64

"Nearly half of the single women in America do not want to get married." This conclusion is from a survey of 1,057 adults conducted by Scripps Howard New Service and Ohio University. Offhand, I'd say those academic eggheads at Ohio University are scrambled. "but two-thirds of the nation's unmarried men hope to tie the knot some day." Somebody up there is manipulating statistics, for sure.

65

"A successful man is one who makes more money than his wife can spend. A successful woman is one who can find such a man."
~ Lana Turner

66

"Women versus Dogs: A Comparative Analysis." Dogs are loyal; they're good companions; they're very forgiving; and they love you *unconditionally*. That's four points for dogs. Women... women... Oh, and dogs also never run off with all your money. Women, on the other hand... well... Dogs, however, always greet you warmly when you return home. Women, well, women... Dogs never talk back, either.

67

"A man may be a fool and not know it—but not if he is married."
~ H.L. Mencken

Behind the Eight Ball

68-73

Romantics send red roses.
Unromantics send excuses.

Romantics call simply to say "I love you."
Unromantics call collect.

Romantics ask "Will you be my Valentine?"
Unromantics ask "When will dinner be ready?"

Romantics get tipsy on champagne.
Unromantics get sloshed on Jim Beam.

Romantics watch *Casablanca*.
Unromantics watch *Rocky Horror Picture Show*.

Romantics watch *An Officer and a Gentleman*.
Unromantics watch *Fatal Attraction*.

74-79

Romantics read *The Bridges of Madison County*.
Unromantics read *The Story of O*.

Romantics buy their girlfriends Godiva chocolates.
Unromantics want their girlfriends to pose as Lady Godiva.

Romantics view romance as the pure expression of affection.
Unromantics view romance as foreplay.

Romantics write love letters.
Unromantics leave messages on her answering machine.

Romantics surprise their spouse with an anniversary dinner.
Unromantics are surprised to discover they're actually married.

80

"Before marriage, a man declares that he would lay down his life to serve you; after marriage, he won't even lay down his newspaper to talk to you."
~ Helen Rowland

Bonnie & Clyde

81-84

Key differences between men and women:

➣ Men read while sitting on the toilet—women don't.
➣ Men play "Air Guitar"—women don't.
➣ Men hear "sex" when you say "romance"—women hear "love."
➣ Men like *The Three Stooges*—women would rather undergo the Chinese water torture.

85

Women do *not* want their men to emulate...

- ✦ Willard Scott
- ✦ Boy George
- ✦ Mr. Rogers
- ✦ David Koresh
- ✦ Gomer Pyle
- ✦ RuPaul

86

Men do *not* want their women to emulate...

- ✧ Morticia Addams
- ✧ Hillary Clinton
- ✧ Edith Bunker
- ✧ Jessica Hahn
- ✧ Roseanne Arnold
- ✧ Joan Rivers

87

Him: *It's not that I'm not romantic. I'm just as romantic as the next guy."*
Her: *That's exactly the problem*

88

A famous exchange between Lady Astor and Winston Churchill:

She: *If you were my husband, Winston, I would put poison in your tea.*
He: *If I were your husband, Nancy, I would drink it.*

89

"In love, women are professionals, men are amateurs.
~ Francois Truffaut

Born Losers

90

How to spot a romantic fool: Anyone with a lovey-dovey personalized license plate. They spent a hundred bucks to tell the whole world that they call each other HONY-BUN. Well I, for one, don't care!

91

The most unromantic large cities in America:
- New York City
- New York City (It's so unromantic it tied itself for second place.)
- Pittsburgh, Pennsylvania
- Cleveland, Ohio
- Los Angeles, California

92

"Marriage: a master, a mistress and two slaves, making in all, two."
~ Ambrose Bierce

93

Unromantic occupations

Meter maid
Lawyer
Department of Motor Vehicles clerk
Proctologist
Gynecologist
Tax auditor
Engineer
Sanitation engineer
Politician
Used car dealer
Insurance salesman

94

"Men have a much better time of it than women; for one thing they marry later; for another thing they die earlier."
~ H.L. Mencken

95

Refuse to throw-out *any* of your old magazines. ("Hey, these old *Playboys*, *Sports Illustrateds*, *National Geographics* may be worth *millions* some day!")

Boston Baked Beans

96

The most unromantic dinner you could possibly make: Macaroni and cheese.

97

Farting. Farting is definitely not romantic. Of course, timing is important here, too. Volume and relative strength are critical factors to consider when weighing just how unromantic a particular fart is. Those of you who are intellectually-minded (and just how many of you would be reading a book like this anyway?!) may want to get a copy of a book called *Fart Proudly*. It's a collection of offbeat writings by Benjamin Franklin. (No kidding!)

98

Heart-shaped pancakes are romantic . . . but Mickey Mouse-shaped waffles are *not*. You can get your very own Mickey Waffler for just $49.95 from the Chef's Catalog! Call 800-424-6255.

99

Romantics drink tea. Unromantics drink coffee.

100

"There is no love sincerer than the love of food."
~ George Bernard Shaw

101

Put lots of ketchup on the gourmet meal she prepared for you.

Bowling For Dollars

102

Bowling. Of *course* bowling is unromantic! The classy team T-shirts. The smelly shoes. The camaraderie. The beer.

103

Golfing vs. bowling—Which is more unromantic? Scholars and scientists have argued this question for ages. One argument is that golfing is more expensive, consumes more time, and players wear goofier clothes. The other argument is that you can bowl year-round, you can play more often because it's less expensive, and the balls are bigger.

104

Actually, I have a friend who is a golfer *and* a bowler. Says his wife left him last year . . . and he didn't notice until last week!

105

Unromantic times at the bar scene: First there were mechanical bulls. Then there was Velcro-Jumping. Then there was Karaoke. And now there's . . . *Bar Sumo*—in which otherwise mature people dress-up in highly-padded suits (picture the Pillsbury Dough Boy) and bounce/slam into each other. *Highly* unromantic!

106

If you have a subscription to *Playboy* . . .
. . . and you're under 25, you're just normal.
. . . and you're over 25, you qualify as an unromantic.

Boys Will Be Boys

107

The most unromantic men's names: Kermit, Felix, and Adolph.

108

Do you think Charles Manson is a romantic name? How about Jim Jones? Or Jack Ruby? Or Ronald Reagan? Or Richard Nixon? If you are unfortunate enough to have the same name as some infamous criminal, psycho or bone-headed president, then you're stuck with a name that's *way beyond* unromantic.

109

*"I know many married men.
I even know a few happily married men. but I don't know one
who wouldn't fall down the first open coal-hole running after
the first pretty girl who gave him a wink."*
~ George Jean Nathan

110

Wear white sox with dress shoes. Wear black sox with sandals.

Brides & Other Insane People

111-116

For grooms: How to make your wedding unromantic. (Contrary to popular opinion, weddings aren't *really* that romantic. Why? Because the bride and her mother are so stressed-out and keyed-up that it takes very little to send them into orbit!) Here are some unromantic tips for grooms:

- Insult your new mother-in-law.
- Get drunk at the reception.
- Dance every dance with the Maid of Honor.
- Cop a feel of your bride whenever the photographer attempts a shot.
- Smush the wedding cake in her face. (This is becoming a true unromantic's tradition at American weddings. Boorishness reigns!)
- Sneak out of the reception to watch the end of the Steeler's game.

117

Most unromantic wedding(s): Earlier this year 92 couples were married in a mass ceremony at the Mall of America, which holds the dubious distinction of being the largest mall in the country.

118

Guys, if you're engaged to a trusting, lovely woman, and you want to give her a dose of reality...ask her to sign a pre-nuptial agreement. (Then stand back and watch the tears flow and the sparks fly!)

119

This should go without saying, but shoplifting on your wedding day is considered by most folks to be rather unromantic. File under "Truth Is Stranger Than Fiction"—this, from an Associated Press story: "PRESTONSBURG, Ky — The honeymoon is over, for 30 days anyway, while Jeannie Jacobs Fouts does time for stealing a wedding dress, the groom's suit, pillows for the ring bearer and a camera to film her wedding. Under a plea bargain, Fouts, 19, and her 23-year-old sister, Betty Thomas, admitted guilt to one count each of shoplifting $1,500 worth of merchandise on her wedding day, March 14, 1992... The wedding was delayed seven hours while the women posted bail. The groom was not charged."

120

"The way to hold a husband is to keep him a little jealous; the way to lose him is to keep him a little more jealous."
~ H.L. Mencken

Burp!

121

Garlic.

122

And if you just can't get enough garlic on your *own*, why not plan to take next year's vacation at the Hudson Valley Garlic Festival, held every year in late August in Saugerties, New York. Call 914-246-6982 for more info.

✦ BURP! ✦

123

Onion bagels.

124

Some people buy romantic travel guides, seeking picturesque locales. Other people buy Hamburger Heaven: The Illustrated History of the Hamburger. Author Jeffrey Tennyson has selected these as the best hamburger joints in the U.S.:

- *Kewpee's Hamburgers*, Lima, Ohio
- *In-N-Out Burger*, Los Angeles, California
- *The Chattaway*, St. Petersburg, Florida
- *The Red Rooster Drive-In*, Brewster, New York
- *The Owl Bar & Cafe*, San Antonio, Texas

125

Unromantic's 7-Course Dinner: A six pack and a pizza.

126

The unromantic's friend: Onions.

127

Burping ain't romantic, right? And carbonated beverages make you burp, right? So why is champagne considered romantic?!

But Seriously, Folks

128-135

The "Proudly Unromantic" are *not* all the same, as some people would have you believe. We are not *all* beer-guzzling, TV-watching sloths. — Some of us drink Scotch, too.

Unromantics follow a variety of different philosophies. Here are a few of them:

- ✓ **The Purely Logical**: They follow the Way of Mr. Spock, shunning emotions as an interruption in their lives of logical intellectualism.
- ✓ **The Totally Lazy**: They follow in the footsteps of Al Bundy, avoiding any kind of work, be it paying work or relationship work.
- ✓ **The Merely Incompetent**: They follow the Way of Homer Simpson, who's bumbling incompetence extends from the nuclear power plant to the home.
- ✓ **The Bewildered**: They view the world as does newspaper columnist Dave Barry, who is continually trying to reconcile himself to a world that contains both beautiful women and boogers.
- ✓ **The Merely Boorish**: Followers of Roseanne Arnold, they make an art out of crassness and obnoxiousness.
- ✓ **The Pig-Headed**: Followers of the Head Pig of Pig-Headedness, Miss Piggy, are always totally and *loudly* convinced that they are right about *everything—especially* when they're wrong.
- ✓ **The Merely Angry**: Any feminist role model will do—from Betty Friedan to Bella Abzug.
- ✓ **The Sports Fan**: The true sports fan has the ability to watch *days* of TV with only brief bathroom breaks and snack runs. He has the flexibility to switch from the non-stop action of basketball to the no-action thrills of televised golf—and fervently believe that he is witnessing something of great importance.

136-140

Selections for your Unromantics Library

- *Real Men Don't Eat Quiche*, by Bruce Feirstein: The unromantic's Bible.
- *Dave Barry's Guide to Marriage and/or Sex*: Hilarious, funny, side-splitting, chuckle-producing—and instructive, too!
- *250 Ways to be Romantic*, by Barry Rosen: This book is good for a laugh—*if* you like bland writing and typos. Also, you can join the "King of Romance Fan Club": For just $25 you get a lifetime membership card, autographed photo, biography of this egomaniac, T-shirt and newsletter. [Who *is* this bozo?!]
- *How to Make Yourself Miserable*, by Dan Greenburg. With chapters like "How to Avoid Deep Romantic Relationships" and "How to Destroy Deep Romantic Relationships," how could you lose?!
- *The Great Divide*, by Daniel Evan Weiss. This book details how females and males really differ. You'll learn critical facts such as: 78% of females wear colored underwear, while only 24% of males do; 98% of senior executives of Fortune 500 companies are men, and only 2% are female; men are in charge of the TV remote control 55% of the time, and women only 45% of the time.

141-143

Books That Should Be Banned

- *Love*, by Leo Buscaglia: This book is to an unromantic as a wooden stake is to Dracula.
- *1001 Ways To Be Romantic*, by Gregory J.P. Godek: This book is to an unromantic as water is to the Wicked Witch of the West. (And what's the deal with the two middle initials, huh?!)
- *Men Are From Mars, Women Are From Venus*, by John Gray, Ph.D. This book is a great disappointment. The title seems to indicate that it will be a rollicking blast of a book. But it's simply another sappy self-help book that tells you how to "communicate" with your partner and be "sensitive." [And, the book is misleading, as scientists have recently discovered that men are actually from Neptune, and women are from the far reaches of the Andromeda Galaxy.)

Cheapskates Unite!

144

Unromantics shun cute little bed and breakfasts in favor of the cheapest roadside motor inn they can find.

145

Wisdom from *Hagar the Horrible*: "Money can't buy happiness. However, in some cases, it can be used as a down payment."

146

Refuse to throw away . . . your old ties . . . your polyester suits . . . your bellbottom pants . . . your collection of college T-shirts.

Co-Dependency for Fun & Profit

147

"Between men and women there is no friendship possible.
There is passion, enmity, worship, love—
but no friendship."
~ Oscar Wilde

148

Everyone knows that having good self-esteem is a prerequisite for being romantic. So, of course, having *poor* self-esteem leads naturally to an unromantic life. This is *obvious*. What I would like to point-out is that good self-esteem is bad for the economy! Think about it... If everyone had good self-esteem, the first thing that would happen is that all the psychiatrists would be out-of-business. Then all the advertising people would be out of a job, because consumers would no longer fall for the advertising gimmick of trying to convince us that we would be sexier/more attractive/healthier/happier if we bought yet one more stupid product. Then, of course, most of the lawyers would go belly-up, because people with self-esteem don't have a need to sue one another at the drop of a hat. Most of the auto industry would fold-up, because people with self-esteem don't need three cars or fancy cars to impress their neighbors. Anyway, I think you can see the domino effect here. If all Americans had good self-esteem, our economy would fall apart, leaving us wide-open to an economic assault by the Japanese and Germans. Oh, sure, we'd have strong self-esteem and we'd be all romantic and everything—but "Made In America" would be a thing of the past. Do you want this to happen??

149

If your partner has gone off the deep end in terms of "working on her self-esteem" or "getting touch with himself"—you can bring him or her down to earth with this truly funny cassette tape by Greg Tamblyn: *The Shootout at the I'm OK You're OK Corral*. Included are songs titled:

- *I Have a Tendency for Codependency*
- *A 90s Kind of Guy*
- *I Drink, Therefore I Am*

Only $10 from TuneTown, P.O. Box 23452, Nashville, TN 37202.

Dangerous Liaisons

150

The *Sports Illustrated* Swimsuit Issue.

151

"Husbands are chiefly good lovers when they are betraying their wives."
~ Marilyn Monroe

152

If you're a masochist, but you just can't stand the pain, here's just the thing for you: "Pain Pals"—a new service that writes personalized S&M letters to you! "You create the scenario and set the mood for a writing relationship that's 'bound' to hook you into one of the most unique and satisfying lifestyles ever!" the company says. Each letter costs $45, with discount rates of $175 for four weekly letters per month; or just $500 for 12 monthly letters per year. Write to P.O. Box 153, Cliffside Park, NJ 07010.

Dear Mr. Unromantic

153

Dear Mr. Unromantic:
Is there any relationship between ethnic background and romantic tendencies?
Signed, *Worried In Warsaw*

Dear Worried:
I'm happy to report that no single ethnic group has the market cornered on romance: You all have an equal chance of being unromantic. I've investigated many reports from around the globe. For example, there is much anecdotal evidence that Italian men are very romantic. But upon closer inspection, I found that for every "Italian Lover," there is one scoundrel and two lawyers. Likewise, while investigating the famous "Latin Lovers," I found a ratio of one lover to two winos and one banker. And even the French, with their "Continental Flair" seem to be comprised of four chain smokers, one wino and three accountants for every "French Lover."

154

Dear Mr. Unromantic:
What about genetics? My parents are both incurable romantics. Am I destined to grow up to be one of "Them"??
Signed, *Scared in Seattle*

Dear Scared:
The battle over "Nature versus Nurture" still rages among scientists and philosophers alike. Frankly, we don't know for sure. My advice is to limit your contact with your parents, and find some role models who are more appropriate, like your local chapter of Hell's Angels, or maybe the local lodge of the Shriners.

155

Dear Mr. Unromantic:
I'm embarrassed to admit this, but I am a closet romantic. On the outside I'm "One of the guys," but on the way home, I sneak into a local florist shop, and buy flowers (pansies—my girlfriend's favorites). I can't seem to help myself. What should I do?
Signed, *Pansy In Pittsburgh*

Dear Pitts:
First, seek counseling. If that doesn't change you, accept yourself as you are and move to California. All kinds of nuts live out there, and your "tendencies" won't stick out as much. Good luck! (And don't write again.)

156

Dear Mr. Unromantic:
My wife has spent my salary for 40 years on shoes. Now she's spending my retirement fund on *hats*. What should I say to her?
Signed, *Frustrated in Fairport*

Dear Frustrated:
"You look lovely, dear."

157

Dear Mr. Unromantic:
My husband is an engineer. He spends more time in his basement workshop tinkering with his bicycle than he does in our bedroom tinkering with me. What should I do?
Signed, *Edgy in Ellington*

Dear Edgy:
There's nothing you *can* do—he's an *engineer*. (Just thank your lucky stars that he's not an *accountant*.)

158

Dear Mr. Unromantic:
I haven't had sex with my husband since he took up golf three years ago. I'm still young, attractive, and interested. How can I get him to be interested in me?
Signed, *Still Sexy in Sudbury*

Dear Sexy:
Try polishing his putter and waxing his balls. This usually assures a hole-in-one.

Deep Freeze

159-163

Unromantic gestures from the pros:

- Socks on the floor.
- Pantyhose on the shower rod.
- Underwear on the bedpost.
- Moldy milk in the refrigerator.
- Dirty dishes in the sink.

164

"The concern that some women show at the absence of their husbands does not arise from their not seeing them and being with them, but from the apprehension that their husbands are enjoying pleasures in which they do not participate, and which, from their being at a distance, they have not the power of interrupting."
~ Montaigne

165-172

Universal Laws:
- Marriage is the alliance of two people, one of whom never remembers birthdays and the other who never forgets them.
  ~ Ogden Nash
- People who sleep with the windows open always marry partners who insist on the windows staying closed.
- Prudes marry perverts.
- Women who love to dance always marry men with two left feet.
  ~ Gregory J.P. Godek
- Fussy, neat people marry slobs.
- Teetotalers marry beer drinkers.
- Joggers marry couch potatoes.
- Intelligent women always marry fools. ~ Anatole France

173

Share an intimate story about the two of you with friends—then say, "Oops, that wasn't *you*, was it."

Deep Throat

174

*"Sex alleviates tension.
Love causes it."*
~ Woody Allen

175

Blow-up sex dolls are about as unromantic as you can get, I suppose. Personally, I think it's kind-of cheating—I mean, where's the challenge in being romantic to a life-sized blow-up Barbie doll? Anyway, in case you're interested, a "Cindy" catalog is available for $5 from Metro Sales, Dept., 311G, box 1381, Studio City, CA 91614.

176

Here is part of a review of the new book *Without Sin: The Life and Death of the Oneida Community*, by Spencer Klaw. (Oneida was a utopian colony founded in the 1850s in upstate New York.) Here's the challenge: Guess which publication this review is from: *Cosmo*, *Penthouse*, *The Wall Street Journal*, or *The Village Voice*.

"Though the Shakers shunned sex, the residents of Oneida luxuriated in it . . . Life at Oneida revolved around the pleasures of the flesh . . . A lot of sex [said the leader of the group] was the will of God. At Oneida, marriage was frowned upon; Noyes believed that marriage 'gives to sexual appetite only a scanty and monotonous allowance.' And so men and women were to 'circulate' sexually, the result being a sort of sexual dos-a-dos, swing your partner round and round and move on to the next . . . Those who fell in love were stigmatized, sometimes sent to satellite colonies, the Oneida equivalents of re-education camps. Sleeping around was the thing, and here a few words from Chairman Noyes may provide the right flavor: 'You may say that you have no taste for anybody but your wife. But your taste may be diseased. God will not have in his kingdom those who cannot love all that he loves.'"

You well-read business executives are *right*! This book review appeared in the *Wall Street Journal* on September 22, 1993. Go figure!

177

"Brevity is the soul of lingerie."
~ Dorothy Parker

178

In the year 100 A.D., publishing history was made with the publication of the *Kama Sutra of Vatsyayana*.

◆ DIAMONDS ARE A GIRL'S BEST FRIEND ◆

179

"There are a number of mechanical devices which increase sexual arousal, particularly in women. Chief among these is the Mercedes-Benz 380SL convertible."
~ P.J. O'Rourke

Diamonds Are a Girl's Best Friend

180

Tiffanys is unromantic. Rolls Royces are unromantic. Why?? Because, as far as I'm concerned, *anything that is obscenely expensive is unromantic.* Neiman Marcus is unromantic. Cartier is unromantic. Mink coats. Rolex watches. Joy Perfume.

181

"I have never hated a man enough to give his diamonds back."
~ Zsa Zsa Gabor

182

If you say "Hey, it's our anniversary—let's *celebrate!*" thinking that a roll in the sack would be a *great* way to celebrate . . . and she says, "Oh, yes! Let's celebrate with a bottle of *Dom Perignon!*" . . . I suggest that you head for the hills.

Divorce—The Ultimate Cure

183

- The current divorce rate: 52%.
- The second marriage divorce rate: 67%.
- The number of over-30 never-married men has tripled since 1970.

184

"The happiest time of anyone's life is just after the first divorce."
~ John Kenneth Galbraith

185

"So, if marriage is so bad, shouldn't I just get divorced?" you might ask. Not so fast, fella! Things might be bad at home, but consider the alternative ... Go hang out for a while at a singles bar on a Saturday night. Watch the macho, insecure guys. Watch the made-up and stuck-up gals. Watch the games, the tension, the drunken haze. And then go home and count your blessings. Even Roseanne Arnold would be a welcome relief after *that* scene.

186

"Divorces are made in heaven."
~ Oscar Wilde

187

"Never go to bed mad. Stay up and fight!"
~ Phyllis Diller

Do's & Don'ts

188

If you *must* buy roses, *don't* buy red ones, don't buy them fresh, and don't deliver them on time.

189

"Love means never having to say you're sorry."
~ Love Story

[Just *thinking* about this sappy movie makes me *nauseous* . . . but it does contain a bit of wisdom for the true unromantic: *Never apologize for anything!*]

190

Never return her calls promptly. Keep her guessing.

191

Read the paper while eating the gourmet meal that she lovingly prepared for you all afternoon. (Watching TV works equally well.)

192-198

Some favorite, all-purpose unromantic lines:

"I told you so!"
"Were you talking to me?"
"Nyuk-nyuk-nyuk!"
"Yeah, right!"
"I have feelings, too, you know."
"Where's the remote control?"
"Yes, dear."

199

Unromantics do not wear bow ties or suspenders. *Ever.*

Doctor Demento

200

Many people think that walking through beautiful autumn leaves is a romantic thing to do. *I don't.* The last time my girlfriend and I walked through some leaves, I shared with her my view that autumn leaves were like the dried, withered, dead skin of a tree that is slowly decomposing all around us. She turned white, agreed with me, and hurried back to the car. See what I mean?

201

Some surprising advice: Guys, *put your woman on a pedestal!* While this *seems* like a romantic strategy, in truth it is not. By putting her on a pedestal, you're effectively treating her like an *object*, not like a real person.

202

I can't think of *anything* less romantic than talking about sex with a stranger on the phone . . . so here, for your edification and entertainment, are some real toll-free sex lines:

1-800-285-KINK
1-800-967-HEAD
1-800-945-PETS
1-800-825-HOTT
1-800-285-ORGY
1-800-688-69ME
1-800-879-SUCK
1-800-274-2on1
1-800-695-TABU

203

And for those of you who would rather have your sex calls charged directly to your phone bill . . .

1-900-786-HOT1
1-900-884-4FUN
1-900-535-JOCK
1-900-646-1on1
1-900-847-2on1
1-900-HOT-4SEX

204

"The happiest moments in any affair take place after the loved one has learned to accommodate the lover and before the maddening personality of either party has emerged like a jagged rock from the receding tides of lust and curiosity."
~ Quentin Crisp

Doctor Doolittle

205

One great strategy for maintaining your unromantic status is to make sure you don't have any "extra" money laying around—that your woman will undoubtedly expect to be spent on flowers and candy and potpourri. How do you make sure you never have any surplus cash? You take-up an expensive and all-consuming hobby, of course! Favorites include golf, coin collecting, restoring classic cars, and boating. These hobbies will all cause irreversible hemorrhaging of the wallet.

206

Selections from the *Unromantics' Dictionary*:

Kissing: Foreplay.

Holding hands: Foreplay.

Dating: 1) Foreplay, 2) Watching football on TV with her instead of with the guys.

Romance: A figment of a woman's imagination.

Flirting: Foreplay.

Communicating: Pretending to listen to her.

Being sensitive: Nodding your head at the appropriate times.

Being non-judgmental: Keeping your *big mouth shut*, even when you know *damn well* she's wrong.

Unconditional love: An impossibility.

Intimacy: Being in the same room together.

Passion: An adolescent affliction, not unlike acne. Luckily, most of us outgrow it.

Romantic dinner: One where you tuck-in your T-shirt.

Love: Means never having to say you're sorry. (Also known as the "Never apologize, never explain" philosophy.)

Valentine's Day: An invention of that sadist, Mr. Hallmark.

Sex: The purpose of life itself.

Love: See "sex."

Doctor Seuss

207

Karaoke fanatics are *not* romantic. They may *appear* to be romantic—as they croon and sway while singing the latest tear-jerker from Whitney Houston... but they're doing it because they have big egos, not big hearts.

208

Sopranos—unromantic
Altos—romantic
Tenors—romantic
Baritones—unromantic
Basses—romantic

209

"Men want a woman whom they can turn on and off like a light switch."
~ Ian Fleming

Doctor Strangelove

210

Top training grounds for unromantics:

- U.S. Naval Academy
- Harvard Business School
- National Organization for Women
- National Rifle Association
- Any high school boys' locker room
- Fraternities

211

Unromantic groups of people:

- Animal rights activists
- Members of MENSA
- Deadheads
- Mimes
- *Rocky Horror Picture Show* groupies
- Trekkers
- Health food fanatics

212

If you don't have time for all that romance nonsense, but still want to make it with the babes, you may want to try a subliminal seduction tape!

Seduction By Mephisto—"Famous subliminal seduction tape! 52 page catalog explains how the Mephisto tape creates a sexual desire for you and eliminates her inhibitions. Other Mephisto tapes stop divorce, excite passion and eliminate rivals." The Mephisto catalog is just $3, from Intimate Treasures, call 415-896-0944, or write to P.O. Box 77902, Dept. 1CS100193, San Francisco, CA 94107.

213

"Being baldpate is an unfailing sex magnet."
~ Telly Savalas

214

We all know that the military ain't exactly a hotbed of romance. But David Chesterfield, of Fort Lee, New Jersey, wants to know which branch of the service is the *least* romantic of all. Well, until last summer, it was the Navy. But the Marines recently moved into first (last?) place with their aborted effort to ban *married* Marines from the service. Their valiant effort was shot down by the bureaucratic fools in Washington. But we commend the Marines for their effort.

Doomed From the Start

215

"Nobody will ever win the battle of the sexes. There's too much fraternizing with the enemy."
~ Henry Kissinger

✤ DOOMED FROM THE START ✤

216

The *average* couple has *plenty* of opportunities for being unromantic. But if you *really* want to increase your opportunities for friction and misunderstandings, get involved in a *cross-cultural* relationship! Some of the most exciting combinations are:

- ♣ Italians & Irish
- ♣ Germans & French
- ♣ Iranian & Polish
- ♣ Southerners & Anybody Else

Reprinted with permission of Tribune Media Services, Inc., Suburban Cowgirls © 1993

217

Of course, marrying someone outside of your religious faith is always good for adding a little controversy to your love affair—especially around Christmastime!

- ✤ Christians & Jews
- ✤ Christians & Catholics
- ✤ Catholics & Golfers
- ✤ Fundamentalist Moslems & Fundamentalist Baptists
- ✤ Mormons & New Agers

218

And never let it be said that I shy away from sensitive issues... The most volatile relationship combinations of all are when you mix different *races*. Some combinations for you to consider:

- Blacks & Whites
- Orientals & Hispanics
- Watusis & Pygmies
- Humans & 'Toons
- Californians & Humans

219

"If ever I marry, it will be on a sudden impulse—as a man shoots himself."
~ H.L. Mencken

220

Wearing a toupee is unromantic. But then again, so is being bald.

Doozies

221

Two great books from a woman's point-of-view, both by Cynthia Heimel:

- *Get Your Tongue Out of My Mouth, I'm Kissing You Goodbye*
- *If You Can't Live Without Me, Why Aren't You Dead Yet?*

222

I'll bet you thought chocolate was romantic, didn't you? Well, the word from our friends at *Ms. Magazine* say—*not!* According to the March/April 1993 issue, chocolate is not a benign sweet, but rather a cruel oppressor of women! "Chocolate has become a source of anguish for the women who consume it and a health hazard for the women who produce it," according to Cat Cox ["Cat"!?!] , who is also the author of a book called Chocolate Unwrapped: The Politics of Pleasure. "The mythical chocolate portrayed by the advertisers conveys an image far removed from the experience of the increasing numbers of women who, in our body-conscious culture, are acknowledging abusive eating patterns."

223

For a romantic/unromantic meal in London, England, visit the McDonald's Restaurant in elegant Hampstead. The tastefully decorated restaurant has a doorman in tie and tails!

224

Good years and bad years:

1920—Women given the right to vote in the 19th Amendment to the U.S. Constitution.
1948—*Sexual Behavior in the Human Male* published by Alfred Kinsey.
1959—*Lady Chatterley's Lover* banned by U.S. Postmaster General.
1970—*Love Story* is a smash hit movie.
1972—*Ms. Magazine* founded by Gloria Steinem.
1972—*The Joy of Sex* published by Alex Comfort.
1976—Presidential candidate Jimmy Carter admits having lusted in his heart.
1987—Presidential candidate Gary Hart withdraws from race after the media reports on his cruise on the yacht *Monkey Business* with Donna Rice.

225

Tell her you're not attracted to young playmates and skinny models—you'd rather have *her*.

226

"Men are those creatures with two legs and eight hands."
~ Jayne Mansfield

Eggheads

227

The unromantics' school of choice: Massachusetts Institute of Technology. At MIT the favorite sports cheer is:

"Gimme an *M!* Gimme an *A!* Gimme an *S!* Gimme another *S!* Gimme an *A!* Gimme a *C!* Gimme an *H!* Gimme a *U!* Gimme an *S!* Gimme an *E!* Gimme a *T!* Gimme another *T!* Gimme an *S!* Gimme an *I!* Gimme an *N!* Gimme an *S!* Gimme a *T!* Gimme an *I!* Gimme a *T!* Gimme a *U!* Gimme a *T!* Gimme an *E!* Gimme an *O!* Gimme an *F!* Gimme a *T!* Gimme an *E!* Gimme a *C!* Gimme an *H!* Gimme an *N!* Gimme an *O!* Gimme an *L!* Gimme an *O!* Gimme a *G!* Gimme a *Y!* —What's that spell?? — Massachusetts Institute of Technology!!" [What a wild bunch!]

228

Golf for intellectuals: *Chess.*

229

A new twist on an old game: *Centre Chess.* It's chess played on a circular board (picture a dart board). Although each piece still moves according to all the old rules, the circular board makes the game faster-paced and more aggressive. *Yow!* Only $32.95 from the MIT Catalog. Call 617-253-4462, or write The MIT Museum Shop, 265 Massachusetts Ave., Cambridge, MA 02139.

✦ EXCUUUUUUUSE MEEEE! ✦

230

"When a woman becomes a scholar there is usually something wrong with her sex organs."
~ Nietzsche

Excuuuse Me!

231

Leave one last square of toilet paper on the roll. Leave one millimeter of milk in the bottom of the carton. Leave the car with one pint of gasoline in the tank.

232

"Absence makes the heart grow fonder"—so don't call her for days at a time.

233

One of the best unromantic dates I ever created was a night of listening to my Tom Lehrer record collection. Bunny and I listened to all three albums: *Songs by Tom Lehrer*, *That Was the Year That Was*, and *An Evening (Wasted) With Tom Lehrer*. Bunny, being a good Catholic girl, was, I think, particularly impressed by *The Vatican Rag*. But I think it was *The Masochism Tango* that sent her screaming out of my apartment.

234

Tell her you're too busy to go shopping/clean the basement/fix the car . . . But when your buddies call, jump up and play a round of golf!

Familiarity Breeds Contempt

235

"My wife and I have separate bedrooms. We eat apart. We take separate vacations. We're doing everything we can to keep our marriage together!"
~ Rodney Dangerfield

236

How you refer to your girlfriend or wife gives a clear indication of whether you're a romantic or an unromantic. Here is a guide for you:

Romantic	Unromantic
My Honey	My Old Lady
Sweetie	Hey, You!
Sugar Pie	Thunder Thighs
Honey	Honey (Depends on your tone of voice)
Bunny	Bitch

237

Love is based on a view of women that is impossible to those who have had any experience with them."
~ H.L. Mencken

Fatal Attraction

238

Some archetypal unromantic personalities:

Mama's boys
Tomboys
Workaholics
Alcoholics
Mothers
Fathers
Men

239

From TV's *Cheers*: Carla talking to Sam: "I just always thought that I'd be the woman you cheated on your wife with. Call me a hopeless romantic!"

240

When you're away, I'm restless, lonely,
Wretched, bored, dejected;
Only here's the rub, my darling dear,
I feel the same when you are here.

~ Samuel Hoffenstein

Faux Pas

241

Wear that tie that she *hates* when meeting her parents for the first time.

242

Give your current fiancé the engagement ring you'd bought for your former fiancé.

243

Another reason why America is the least romantic country on earth: In the U.S., there are nearly 300 lawyers for every 100,000 people. In Japan there are 12 lawyers per 100,000 people.

244

Suggestion for an unromantic vacation trip: Visit one of the dozens of spectacular caves around America. Caves are mysterious, wet, cold, clammy, and—best of all—they're filled with *bats*. No *wonder* they're so popular with tourists! For a directory of caves, write to the National Caves Association, Route 9, Box 106, McMinnville, TN 37110.

245

In an effort to create an unromantic environment in your home, I recommend velvet paintings. The subject matter is not nearly as important as the medium. When it comes to velvet paintings, there's little difference between bullfighting scenes, Elvises and fruit.

♦ FOR MARRIEDS ONLY ♦

246-249

Wearing T-shirts with stupid sayings on them is truly unromantic. Your partner won't want to admit to knowing you, much less want to hold your hand! Some favorites:

- "Why can't I be rich instead of good looking?" ($12.98)
- "It's not a beer belly—It's a fuel tank for a sex machine." ($12.98)
- "51% Sweetheart. 49% Bitch. Don't push me!" ($12.98)
- "It takes a lot of *balls* to golf the way I do!" ($15.98)

From the *Funny Side Up* catalog: Call 215-361-5130; or write 425 Stump Rd., P.O. Box 2800, North Wales, PA 19454.

For Marrieds Only

250

"Marriage is a great institution.
But I'm not ready for an institution."
~ Mae West

251

According to that expert on marital relations, Andy Capp, "A husband is the legally appointed audience for his missus."

252

Definition:
Wedding ring: The world's smallest handcuffs.

✦ FOR MARRIEDS ONLY ✦

253

For married women: Legally have your last name changed back to your maiden name. Note: The longer you've been married, the madder it will make your husband.

254-257

"Marriage is a bribe to make a housekeeper think she's a householder."
~ Thornton Wilder

"A sacrament by virtue of which each imparts nothing but vexations to the other."
~ Balzac

"Rape by contract."
~ Michelet

"Marriage is a bargain, and somebody has to get the worst of the bargain."
~ Helen Rowland

For Men Only

258

Reasons to not even *bother* being romantic...

- Fear that all women are like Roseanne Arnold.
- The movie *Fatal Attraction*.
- All that "penis envy" stuff. (It gives me the *willies*.)

259-264

Unromantic role models for men:

- Sam Malone
- Dave Barry
- Mr. Ed
- John Belushi
- Curly, Larry & Moe (& Shemp)
- Groucho, Harpo & Chico (& Zeppo)
- Doogie Houser
- Eddie Murphy

265

Beards are unromantic, according to the vast majority of the women surveyed. Kissing a guy with an average beard "feels like rubbing your face in the bristles of a broom." Guys with white fluffy beards remind women of Santa Claus, and he ain't exactly romantic.

266

Mustaches, too, are viewed with suspicion by most women. In a word association test, these are the most common responses to the word *mustache*: Hitler; Used car salesman; Snideley Whiplash.

267

Guys, if you're fed-up with women whining that they're the abused, powerless sex, run out and grab a copy of Warren Farrell's book *The Myth of Male Power*. It argues that men—not women—are the overworked, under appreciated, disposable sex. "If men have all the power," Farrell said, "then why do they now die seven years earlier than women, as opposed to just one year earlier in 1920? If they have power why do they commit suicide four times as frequently as women?"

268

"Bachelors know more about women than married men. If they didn't, they'd be married, too."
~ H.L. Mencken

For Women Only

269-271

Reasons to not even *bother* being romantic . . .

- ♣ Testosterone.
- ♣ The Dallas Cowboys.
- ♣ ESPN

272

Unromantic role models for women:

- ♦ Roseanne Arnold
- ♦ Madonna
- ♦ Sinead O'Connor
- ♦ Lucille Ball
- ♦ Maude
- ♦ The Wicked Witch of the West
- ♦ Roseanne Rosanadanna

♦ FOR WOMEN ONLY ♦

273

This is for real: "Free book explains superiority of women, why men are immature. Enclose two stamps. Christian Home, P.O. Box 37-8498, Chicago, IL 60637." (From a classified ad in *Cosmo*.)

274

Apparently, a lot of women want to go skiing with their own kind . . . that is, without men. Sounds unromantic to me! These are all for real:

❋ Women's Ski Discovery, Sugarbush, Vermont: 802-583-2381
❋ Women's Ski Seminars, Breckenridge, Colorado: 303-453-1643
❋ Women's Week, Stowe, Vermont: 802-253-3000
❋ Women's Ski Weeks, Tahoe, California: 916-583-4232

275

Men and Other Reptiles—a book of witty, nasty and outrageous quotes about men, by Mae West, Margaret Mead, Hepburn and others.

276

For engaged women: Refuse to take his last name when you get married.

277

Faking orgasm. Definitely an unromantic thing to do.

278

"The first-rate woman is a realist. She sees clearly that the world is dominated by second-rate men."
~ H.L. Mencken

Funny Business

279-288

Top 10 Unromantic Professions

1. Ornithologist (Bird watcher)
2. Entomologist (Bug scientist)
3. Lawyer (Leech)
4. Accountant (Bean counter)
5. Gynecologist (No comment)
6. Writer (Egotist)
7. Politician (Professional liar)
8. Televangelist (Money machine)
9. Engineer (Professional nerd)
10. Librarian (Bo-o-o-oring!)

289-294

Romantics tie the knot.
Unromantics tie each other to the bedposts.

Romantics share their deepest secrets.
Unromantics share their social diseases.

Romantics study *1001 Ways To Be Romantic*.
Unromantics study *50 Ways To Leave Your Lover*.

Romantics go ballroom dancing
Unromantics go slam dancing.

Romantics spend Sunday in the park with their lovers.
Unromantics spend all their money on Lottery tickets.

Romantics write heartfelt love letters.
Unromantics write checks that bounce.

295

A business tip from the Marketing Genius of the 20th Century, Madonna: "Losing my virginity was a career move."

Gal Stuff

296

If you *really* want to embarrass your man in public, just call him by one of your pet names in front of his friends. The guys will be calling him "Cute Buns" or "Mr. Ding Dong" for years to come.

297

"The only good husbands stay bachelors: they're too considerate to get married."
~ Finley Peter Dunne

298

"Being a woman is a terribly difficult trade, since it consists principally of dealing with men."
~ Joseph Conrad

Games People Play

299

"Marriage is hardly a thing that one can do now and then—except in America."
~ Oscar Wilde

300-303

A Love Quiz

1. **How does a man say "I love you"?**
   a) He remembers Valentine's Day.
   b) He lets her hold the TV remote control.
   c) He doesn't.
   d) What was the question??

2. **How does a woman *want* a man to say "I love you"?**
   a) With diamonds.
   b) With pearls.
   c) With furs.
   d) With cute little "Love Notes" written on Post-It pads.

3. **How does a woman say "I love you"?**
   a) She wears special perfume.
   b) She sends you sappy greeting cards.
   c) She watches football with you, even though she hates it.
   d) She says "I love you."

4. **How does a man *want* a woman to say "I love you"?**
   a) By cooking his favorite dinner.
   b) By wearing a garter belt, stockings and high heels.
   c) By having sex anywhere, anytime with him.
   d) All of the above.

304-306

Dressing like an unromantic.
While there is no *definite* way to recognize an unromantic simply by the way he or she dresses, here are some guidelines.

- ❒ Unromantics prefer last year's (or last decade's) fashions to whatever's hot *this* season.
- ❒ Unromantic men like T-shirts and unpolished shoes.
- ❒ Unromantic women *never* wear high heels—they wear Birkenstocks.

307

The Token Effort
Helping around the house can be romantic. But making a token effort is *not* romantic. The truly *skilled* unromantic knows how to time his offer so that: 1) He gets points for asking, 2) But his partner is nearly done with the chore, so she says, "Oh, that's okay, don't bother."

308-310

Any game that involves self-disclosure is a sure-fire set-up for a fight. Even—or *especially*—the games that promise romance and communication. So be prepared! Games to watch for:

- *How to Host a Romantic Evening*—"Encourages intimacy and meaningful communication long after the game is over." [Yeah, *right*!]
- *Scruples*—The game with fun and enlightening questions like "If you could have an affair and be certain never to be caught, would you do it?" [Now *this* is what I call *fun*!]
- *LifeStories*—"An easy and fun way to get several generations talking and laughing together." [Why not make the *whole family* angry and resentful?! "Hey Jim, tell the story about weird Uncle Ernie! Or how about Aunt Ginnie's secret that her husband is really gay. —*Oops*!"

Garter Belts Galore!

311

According to a survey conducted by The Cooper Marketing Group, of Oak Park, Illinois, men tend to buy bright red and black lingerie as gifts; they think women like it as much as they do. Women, as you might have guessed, prefer lingerie that's white, beige or pale pink.

❧ GARTER BELTS GALORE! ❧

312-316

Here are just a few of the catalogs available from Intimate Treasures, a supplier of many catalogs—some romantic and some... well, *you* decide.

- ☛ *Domina*—"Submit to the hottest collection of provocative Euro-designed PVC fashions for the well-dressed individualist."
- ☛ *Leather For Lovers*—"The hottest collection of sexy leather accouterments ever assembled. Garter belts, rings, slings—more than we dare mention!"
- ☛ *Dream Dresser*—"Fashion fetish fantasy clothing. The most elite catalog available to the erotic shopper. Lingerie of leather, rubber... 5" and 6" stiletto heel shoes and boots, open breast costumes, corsets, fabulous dresses."
- ☛ *Good Vibrations*—"This one's different. Our tasteful, irreverent and informative catalog features the highest quality vibrators, oils, dildoes and more. Woman-owned and operated.
- ☛ Also—*The Sexuality Library*: Books and videos about sex that won't insult your intelligence. From electrifying erotica to enlightening advice."

All of these intriguing catalogs are available from Intimate Treasures, P.O. Box 77902, Dept. 1CS100193, San Francisco, CA 94107; or call 415-896-0944.

317

Fact: Garter belt sales at Frederick's of Hollywood increased by 50% after the 1986 release of the movie *Bull Durham*. Go figure!

318

Keep the *Playboy Playmates Calendar* on your desk at home. Keep a *Snap-on Tools Calendar* on the wall in the garage. (You can get one for only $12. Write to Snap-on Tools, 2801 80th St., Kenosha, WI 53141.)

319

Spiked heels in a water bed.

Go Ahead, Make My Day!

320

Unromantic Story of the Week, from *USA Today*: "Leigh-Anne Csuhany (a.k.A. Mrs. Kelsey Grammer) says she'd "trade anything to get him back." Kelsey Grammer, that is. TV's *Frasier* is seeking to annul the eight-month marriage saying it was based on fraud; he didn't know she was of "unsound mind."

"Two weeks before we were married there was an incident at our home," the former topless dancer tells *Inside Edition*. "I ended up getting arrested and charged with spousal abuse." Csuhany admits when she gets "frustrated . . . angry, I can't stop myself from flipping out. I'd throw things and I'd scream and yell. I have a chemical imbalance, but I take . . . Prozac, that helps me great." Three months pregnant when Grammer asked for an annulment, Csuhany attempted suicide, and miscarried. "I hate him for that. No, I don't hate him, I love him," she says. "I'm still hanging on to the hair of hope."

Good luck, kids.

321

Another unromantic vacation stop: The Typewriter Museum. Housed in the headquarters of the National Office Machine Dealers Association, the museum features rare typewriters from the mid-1800s. You'll find them in beautiful downtown Kansas City, Missouri.

322

Unromantic advice to men: *Give advice to your wife.* Most women are too shy to ask for your advice, so go ahead and give it freely and often. Favorite topics: 1) How you can improve your efficiency in performing basic household tasks, 2) How you should dress, to look more like that pretty little thing who just moved-in down the street, 3) How you can be a better driver.

323

Unromantic advice to women: *Nag your husband.* Even though he will deny it, he values your input. Your constant nagging is proof that you still care. Favorite topics: 1) Why don't you make more money? 2) Why don't you lose some weight? 3) You aren't the same man I married.

Going Bonkers

324

I'll grant you that poetry *can* be romantic. But most of it is either sentimental rubbish or just plain *unintelligible*. Take, for example, this love sonnet by William Shakespeare:

> *Your love and pity doth th' impression fill,*
> *Which vulgar scandal stamped upon my brow;*
> *For what care I who calls me well or ill,*
> *So you o'er-green my bad, my good allow?*

What the *hell* does *this* mean?? If this is what romance is all about, no *wonder* so many relationships are screwed-up: *Nobody knows what they're talking about!*

325

Ninety-four percent of men surveyed report that taking a *Cosmo Quiz* with their girlfriends resulted in a major fight—not the closeness promised in the quiz.

326

Seventy-eight percent of men surveyed report that they believe the letters in Penthouse Forum are true. The remaining 28 percent *wish* they were true—for *them*.

327

If you long for the romance of the medieval days—you're *nuts*! They're not called The Dark Ages for nothing, you know. It was an age characterized by ignorance and disease, not by King Arthur and his mythical knights. Anyway, if you really enjoy jokers dressed like fools, and fake jousting tournaments, then by all means, visit one of the nation's many medieval festivals. The King Richard's Faire is held every year in early September in Carver, in eastern Massachusetts. Call 508-866-5391 for more info.

328

Snoring. Most unromantic guys—and a few of the women—snore. We don't know exactly why. The unromantic scientists insist that it's a purely physiological phenomenon. The romantic scientists are convinced that it's proof that the unconscious mind is still obnoxious, even when the conscious mind is sleeping.

★ GOLF ★

Golf & Other Unromantic Stuff

329

I *know* that your wife can't enjoy watching you on the golf course (—*somebody* has to work, care for the kids, and clean the house!) . . . but now you can share some of golf's hilarious moments with the new videotape *Birdies and Bloopers*. A full half hour of bloopers and shenanigans by the pros (Palmer, Nicklaus, Trevino, Amy Alcott, Lopez). Only $14.98! From the *Funny Side Up* catalog: Call 215-361-5130; or write 425 Stump Rd., P.O. Box 2800, North Wales, PA 19454.

330

The only way most golfers will ever get a hole-in-one . . . is if they make love with their partner on the 9th green.

331

The Bare Facts of Golf—the video! "Golf instruction is beautifully demonstrated by the amply endowed Kathy Piet, in a humorous and most entertaining manner. You'll learn about grips, proper alignment, putting, reading the green and much more. Partial nudity." Only $19.98 from the *Playboy Catalog*. Call 800-423-9494; or write *Playboy Catalog*, P.O. Box 809, Itasca, IL 60143.

332

With a little creativity, you can make nearly *anything* unromantic. Take a simple game of *Monopoly*. First, you could become a Monopoly *fanatic*, playing the game as often as some guys play golf. Second, you don't play for fun, you play to *win*—you play like Donald Trump on speed. And third, you don't play on just any Monopoly board. No, no, *no*! You invest $495 in the Monopoly Collector's Edtion! This exclusive from Franklin Mint features "architecturally designed houses and hotels die-cast and accented with sterling silver or gold . . . a fine hardwood playing surface . . . double the usual supply of money" and nifty drawers built into the playing board for stashing your money and real estate portfolios! I'm excited just *thinking* about it! Write to The Franklin Mint, Franklin Center, PA 19091.

333

Baseball caps are truly unromantic. They can take a handsome, romantic-looking guy, and make him look like a dork in an instant. (Bonus Points for wearing it *backwards*.)

Gone With the Wind

334

*"They have a right to work wherever they want—
as long as they have dinner ready when you get home."*
~ John Wayne

335

Remember: Love is just a series of random chemical reactions in the brain.

336

The Shortest Yet Least Romantic Movie of All Time: *Bambi Meets Godzilla*. [This is a *real* movie.]

337

"I like long walks—especially when they are taken by people who annoy me."
~ Fred Allen

Good Grief!

338

After your partner has shared her deepest feelings about something that's troubling her, these are the phrases that she *least* wants to hear:

- "Don't have a cow, man!"
- "You eediot!"
- "You talkin' to *me*?!"
- "So what's for dinner?"

339

Buy a copy of *1001 Ways To Be Romantic*, by Gregory J.P. Godek, and do the exact *opposite* of everything in the book! [What do you think "J.P." stands for, anyway?]

340

"No good deed goes unpunished."
~ Folk saying

341

And then there are *some* activities—I'm reluctant to call them "hobbies"—that are so... so odd, pointless, and/or weird that they place a person out beyond the furthest reaches of "unromance" and into the Twilight Zone. Such are the members of the International Brick Collectors' Association. These folks are fascinated by the collection, history, manufacture and technological aspects of *bricks*. If you are so afflicted, contact the association at 80 E. 106th Terrace, Kansas City, MO 64114.

342

Another good way to waste your money: Get romantic advice from the Psychic Hotline. Only $1.99 per minute! Call 900-740-5656.

Guy Stuff

343

The unromantics' altar: The toolbench.

344

The unromantics' alternate altar: The computer.

345

The unromantics' cathedral: 1) The garage, 2) The basement.

346

How to Date Young Women: For Men Over 35, by R. Don Steele. Some selections from the Table of Contents:

- ✘ *Understand Her*: The typical 20 year old. Her agenda. What she knows about sex. Her motives for dating you. Understanding all 18-24 year olds.
- ✘ *Get Ready for Her*: Young friends. Back to school. Your place.
- ✘ *Date Her*: Accidental dates. Pseudo dates. How to get a pseudo date. When she doesn't agree.

For more info, call or write Steel Balls Press: 800-428-5992; Box 807, Whittier, CA 90608.

347

"It is impossible to make love to every woman—but one must try."
~ Pushkin

Gym Class

348

Unromantic participation sport #1: *Running*. It costs little, yet takes lots of time. You can start at any level and work your way up to marathons. It gets you out of the house morning, noon and/or night. {Thanks to B./J. E.}

349

Unromantic participation sport #2: *Bicycling*. Actually, bicyclists spend more time disassembling and assembling their bikes than *riding* them, but that only makes the sport more time-consuming (not to mention *irritating* to their partners).

350

Running—unromantic
Walking—romantic
Weight lifting—unromantic
Racquetball—unromantic
Bicycling—unromantic
Rollerblading—unromantic
Ice skating—unromantic
Skating on thin ice—unromantic
Basketball—unromantic
Tennis—romantic
Skiing—romantic
Badminton—romantic . . . foolish, but romantic
Croquet—see "badminton"
Aerobics—unromantic
Swimming—unromantic

Happiness Is a Warm Gun

351

"My husband and I have never considered divorce . . . murder, sometimes, but never divorce."
~ Dr. Joyce Brothers

352-356

More unromantic role models:

☆ Morton Downey, Jr.
☆ Jimmy Swaggart
☆ H.L. Mencken
☆ Roseanne Arnold
☆ Richard M. Nixon

357

❋ Romantics drive BMWs.
❋ Unromantics drive pick-up trucks.

358

➤ Romantics support the NOW.
➤ Unromantics support the NRA.

Happy Anniversary

359-370

In an effort to balance the Hallmark-created pseudo holidays like Valentine's Day, Sweetest Day and National Woodpecker Appreciation Day, here are some *unromantic* dates to mark on your calendar. (These are *real* events, sponsored by *real* people):

January 4—*Trivia Day*
February 14-21—*National Condom Week*
March 1—*National Pig Day*
April 26—*Hug An Australian Day*
May 1—*Law Day*
June 6—*National Yo-Yo Day*
July 3—*Air Conditioning Appreciation Day*
August 5-11—*National Video Game Week*
September 5—*Be Late For Something Day*
October 14—*National Frump Day*
November 19—*Have a Bad Day Day*
December 21—*Humbug Day*

✦ HAPPY ANNIVERSARY ✦

371-380

Unromantic suggestions for celebrating your anniversaries:

1st—Go golfing
2nd—Celebrate with champagne (get blasted)
3rd—Go golfing
4th—Take her to dinner (at McDonald's)
5th—Play poker with the guys
6th—Buy her lingerie (a peek-a-boo bra & crotchless panties)
7th—Be away on a business trip
8th—Play golf
9th—Let *her* be in charge of the TV remote control
10th—Give her a hundred bucks to buy a present for herself

Reprinted with permission of King Features Syndicate, Sally Forth © 1993

381-393

Classic unromantic gifts:

- Fondue pots
- Blenders
- Electric brooms
- Toasters
- Motor oil
- Socket wrenches
- Power tools

- Dust mops
- McDonald's coupons
- Wisk brooms
- Vacuum cleaners
- Weed whackers
- Salad shooters

1001 WAYS *NOT* TO BE ROMANTIC

Ho-Ho-Ho!

394

National statistics show that women outlive men by nearly seven years. (The average life expectancy for women is 78.9 years, compared with 72 years for men.) These numbers are often used to point-out the supposed superiority of women. Has anyone ever considered that the reason men die sooner is that *we have to put up with women for all of those years?!*

395

I've asked many women if they think bedroom ceiling mirrors are romantic. Forty-five percent of them roll their eyes, 50% of them walk away without bothering to answer, and 5% of them slap my face.

You can get a lightweight, 52" x 40" ceiling mirror for only $12.95 from The Stamford Collection, P.O. Box 1160, Dept. KA-32, Long Island City, NY 11101.

396

Cars with bucket seats and stick shifts may be sporty, but they're *not* romantic. Have you ever tried to make-out with your honey, lean over, and get that stick shift right up your . . . ?

397

Have you ever heard this one? "Oh, honey—let's go cut our own Christmas tree together! It will be *so-o-o* romantic!" What do you do? You go along, of course. Because the *reality* of the situation is that Christmas tree cutting is among the Number One Things That Couples Fight About During The Holidays. You hop in your car, full of anticipation and the jolly spirit of the season. You return with a scraggly yet expensive evergreen strapped to the roof of your car, which is where you wish your partner were riding.

398

"One of the aims of connubial bliss is to punish both parties."
~ H.L. Mencken

Home Alone

399

Proof that humans are evolving and getting smarter: "Historically, 95 percent of all Americans got married at least once in their lives. The Census bureau now estimates that number has dropped to about 90 percent, and could decline even more." (From a *Scripps Howard News Service* story.)

400

Fun facts: The number of un-remarried, divorced people has tripled since 1970.

401

What kind of dogs do unromantics own?

* Poodles—romantic
* Boxers—unromantic
* Collies—romantic
* German Shepherds—unromantic
* Great Danes—unromantic
* Pit bulls—king of the unromantics
* Beagles—romantic
* Mutts—unromantic
* Golden retrievers—romantic
* Scottish terriers—romantic
* Greyhounds—unromantic
* Dachshund—romantic

402

Keep your high school football trophies prominently displayed on the fireplace mantle—regardless of what her expensive interior designer recommends. (They're just *jealous*, anyway.)

403

If you don't happen to be a "handyman" type of guy, but you still want to turn your basement into your private hideaway, buy a pool table.

Homer Simpson, Revisited

404

Unromantics believe that . . . PC stands for "Partly Cloudy."

405

Unromantics believe that . . . they are *always* right. Therefore, what's the point of listening to your partner?

406

Unromantics believe that . . . they are God's gift to the opposite sex.

407

Unromantics believe that . . . "communication" is for people who can't handle silence.

408

Unromantics believe in . . . being genuine—even if they have to fake it.

Honey, I Blew Up the Relationship

409

Portable telephones and electronic beepers are *great* for interrupting any potentially romantic situation. Make sure you leave them turned on, and keep them near-by.

410

Unless your wife or girlfriend is a Playboy bunny or a busty 17-year-old, a great way to make her feel inadequate and embarrassed is to take her out to dinner at a Hooters Restaurant, with its sexist puns and nubile waitresses. ("More Than a Mouthful" . . . "Good clean fun" my *ass*!)

411

What I've learned from 30-some years of reading *Dear Abby*: If you truly want to drive a woman *insane*, do these two things: 1) Leave the toilet seat up, and 2) Put the roll of toilet paper on the roller the opposite way from how she prefers it!

412

"Know thine enemy." Lao Tse—or Plato—or was it Sylvester Stallone?—who said this? Anyway, it's good advice. The true unromantic occasionally skims through a copy of *Cosmo*, *Lears* or whatever trash your partner happens to read. Why?! —How do you expect to know what the enemy is thinking unless you read what she's reading?

For example: Let's say this month's Cosmo has an article titled "Multiple Orgasms: Every Woman's Right!" (and *every* issue seems to have one such article). What does this mean to you? It means that you're going to have to prepare some defense against this new expectation! [My panel of experts suggests headaches, poker, or bad breath.]

413

"The only solid and lasting peace between a man and his wife is, doubtless, a separation."
~ Lord Chesterfield

Honeymoon Hell

414

Non-Romantic Honeymoon Destination #202: Disneyland. I can't *imagine* a less romantic setting than a glorified carnival with life-sized cartoon characters chasing screaming children through spotless streets.

415

Non-Romantic Honeymoon Destination #99: Niagara Falls. Took my first wife there. She became obsessed with the fear that she'd left the bathtub running in our apartment. I became obsessed with finding the nearest restroom.

416

If volcanoes make you hot—or if your honey is just a hopeless geologist—take a vacation to the peninsula of Kamchatka in the far-eastern edge of Russia. With 30 active volcanoes plus lava flows, thermal pools and black sand, Kamchatka is a volcano-lover's delight! The Planetary Society of Pasadena, California (those romantic devils) run a 10-day tour every August. Cost is only $3,000! Note: The tour is limited to 20 people, so it's bound to fill-up fast! Call 800-969-6277.

417

Veteran vacationers are always leery of the lodging descriptions in travel guides. Here's a sad tale reported by the *New York Times News Service*: "The guidebook described the inn as a former private estate with 'beautiful courtyards, narrow brick paths and adobe archways' near the heart of Santa Fe, N.M. Guest rooms, the description read, had a "fireplace, Navajo rugs and other regionally crafted art.' At $135 a night, the price wasn't exactly cheap, but it wasn't bad, either, for what was described as a suite in a historic estate. Reality presented a wholly different picture. The 'suite' was a kitchenette in dire need of major renovation. The 'beautiful courtyard' was in fact a large, gravel parking lot. The only rugs were of the fuzzy bath mat variety . . . The 'regionally crafted art' turned out to be a couple of mass-produced clay figures from Mexico."

The lesson, as far as I can see, is simply to stay at home. At least you know exactly what's going to be on TV.

Hooters!

418

Whenever she says "I love you," answer with "Ditto."

419

From the Unromantics' Hall of Fame

Dear Abby reports that one woman's husband handed her a check and said: "Listen, I hate to shop, so this is for your birthday, anniversary, Christmas and Mother's Day, for the next five years."

420

"Women have to be twice as good as men at everything.
Fortunately this is not difficult."
~ Charlotte Whitton

421

High up on every guy's list of unpleasant surprises is discovering that your new girlfriend is wearing . . . a padded bra.

422

High up on every *gal's* list of unpleasant surprises is discovering that your new *boyfriend* is wearing . . . a padded bra.

How To Ruin Your Life

423

Unromantic places to go on a date:

- ☐ **The zoo.** The monkeys are always doing very embarrassing things. A really lousy first date. Unless you're kind-of strange.
- ☐ **The planetarium.** Who do you think you are, Carl Sagan? "Billions and *billions* of ways to bore your partner!"
- ☐ **The movies.** You pay an outrageous amount to get in. You pay a king's ransom for some lousy popcorn. And then you get to sit side-by-side, not interacting for 2 to 3 hours, all the while thinking about either copping a feel or about how much you have to go to the bathroom. Fun, huh?!
- ☐ **The circus.** Clowns ain't romantic.

424

How to ruin your life. Take up golf.

425

"Adultery is the application of democracy to love."
~ H.L. Mencken

426

The most annoying, least romantic instruments you could possibly take-up (presented in descending order, with the least romantic first):

- ❖ Bagpipes
- ❖ Accordion (running a *very* close second)
- ❖ Harmonica
- ❖ Bassoon
- ❖ Triangle
- ❖ Flute-O-Fone
- ❖ Harpsicord

427

Guys: Wear short sox, so that when you cross your legs, three inches of your hairy legs are exposed. Women just *hate* this!

I Can't Get No (Satisfaction)

428

Blind dates are, *by definition*, unromantic. They are the most uncomfortable, stressful encounters ever devised by married people for the torture of their single friends.

429

Women *love* to see men in tuxedos. This is true. —But *not* for the reason you think. It's not because they're so "romantic." It's because men squirm uncomfortably in tuxes—and women love to see men suffer and squirm. I think that women invented tuxedos as revenge for the invention of the chastity belt, back in the Middle Ages. Think about it: What man in his right mind would voluntarily put on a ridiculous bow tie, wear a shirt with ruffles or ridges and little pointy collar-things, and then strap-on a *cummerbund*??

430

Warning! Warning! Remove from your album or CD collection these selections:

- *Breathless*, by Kenny G
- *Shepherd Moons*, by Enya
- *Wintersong*, by Paul Winter
- *Down to the Moon*, by Andreas Vollenweider
- *Valley in the Clouds*, by David Arkenstone
- *Autumn*, by George Winston
- *Heartstring*, by Earl Klugh

431-435

... And replace those offending albums with these selections:

- *Sheer Heart Attack*, by Queen
- *Bat Out of Hell*, by Meatloaf
- Anything by Madonna
- *Nurds*, by The Roaches
- Soundtrack from *2001: A Space Odyssey*
- *Quadrophenia*, by The Who

436

"All young men greatly exaggerate the difference between one young woman and another."
~ George Bernard Shaw

I Was Just Thinking...

437

A fine French wine is a romantic classic. And California wines ain't bad either. But did you know that wine is also produced in *Cleveland* and *New Jersey*? Those are not the first locations that spring to mind when you think *romance*, are they?? Frankly, I tend to think urban decay, the Mafia, and hazardous chemical waste. Be that as it may... If you'd like to sample some wines from these locales, I would suggest Chalet Debonne Vineyards, outside Cleveland, at 216-466-3485, and Four Sisters Winery, in northern New Jersey, at 908-475-3671.

338

"You see an awful lot of smart guys with dumb women, but you hardly ever see a smart woman with a dumb guy."
~ Erica Jong

439

Eating lots of garlic is a great way to keep your lover at arm's length for three to four days.

440

The namesake for our modern celebration of love, Saint Valentine, was a Christian martyr who suffered a horrible death at the hands of the Romans in c270 AD. This is romantic??

441

"Girls have an unfair advantage over men: if they can't get what they want by being smart, they can get it by being dumb."
~ Yul Brynner

442

Let's get one thing straight: Valentine's Day is *not* a holiday. —Nobody gets the day off work (not even the Post Office workers or Federal Bureaucrats). And it's not a "Season," either, the way Christmas is the "Holiday Season." [This has been a public service message from your Uncle Joe, to help keep this romantic-thing from getting out of hand!]

I'm Dysfunctional, You're Dysfunctional

443

As one grows older, one *naturally* becomes less romantic. It's the Natural Order of Things. So don't fight it! Here's an overview of the stages we go through as we age:

Age	Developmental Stage
0-2	Ignorance
3-9	Innocence
10-17	Idealism
18-22	Romance
23-28	Optimism
29-40	Realism
41-49	Pessimism
50-52	Confusion
53-55	Re-Evaluation
56-64	Cynicism
65-69	Retirement
70+	Resignation

444

"It's better to have a lame excuse than none at all."
~ Anonymous

445

"Finding yourself," improving your self-esteem, or going into counseling are all sure-fire ways to kill romance. People who "find themselves" usually lose their partners in the process. People who improve their self-esteem often realize that they deserve much better than their current partner, so they split. And going to counseling... well—those who open a can of worms get what they deserve!

446

"I could be content that we might procreate like trees, without conjunction, or that we were any way to perpetuate the world without this trivial and vulgar way of coition; it is the foolishest act a wise man commits in all his life."
~ Sir Thomas Browne

If God Had Meant Man to be Romantic...

447

If God had meant man to be romantic... He never would have invented golf.

448

If God Had Meant Man to be Romantic... He never would have invented football.

449

If God Had Meant Man to be Romantic... He never would have invented TV.

450

"My mom said that the only reason men are alive is for lawn care and vehicle maintenance."
~ Tim Allen

451

"Women aren't embarrassed when they buy men's pajamas, but a man buying a nightgown acts as though he were dealing with a dope peddler."
~ Jimmy Cannon

Immaturity & Other Techniques

452

Giggle through the romantic scenes in movies.

453

I *hate* Garfield. Even though Garfield is truly unromantic, I *hate* Garfield. I *know* that a Garfield T-shirt makes women think you're an idiot. I *know* that the stuffed Garfields that stick on your car windows prove that your a sophomoric buffoon. I *know* that women feel that Garfield watches, pins, coffee mugs, underwear, posters, bed sheets and wallpaper are more fitting of children than of grown men. But I *still* hate Garfield.

454

"In the sex-war, thoughtlessness is the weapon of the male, vindictiveness of the female."
~ Cyril Connolly

455

Practical jokes. Practical jokes are a *great* way to practice your creativity, stay in touch with the child inside you, and annoy your partner—all at the same time!

In-Laws & Other Household Pests

456

One surefire way to kill your romance, or at least seriously wound it, is to invite your mother to live with you. [I don't really need to elaborate on this one, do I?!]

457-462

Unromantic pets:

- Pit bulls
- Mice
- Piranhas
- Snakes
- Mushrooms
- Ferrets

463

Thinking of getting her a cute little kitten or maybe a puppy for Christmas? Why not *really* surprise her—with a baby *ostrich*?! These big, ugly but fast birds are becoming increasingly popular, according to the American Ostrich Association. (But then, what do you *expect* them to say?) For more information about these amazing birds, write to the association at 3840 Hulen St., Suite 210, Ft. Worth, TX 76107.

Inappropriate Gestures

464

Eventually, every man is faced with a crucial and unavoidable question: "Should you—or should you not—open doors for women?" Some women want you to be "gentlemanly"—while other women want to be treated as equals, and are *insulted* if you open a door for them. My solution?—I sidestep the whole issue: I just stand there and let *them* open the door for *me!*

465

Candid Polaroid photos of her in bed... a classically unromantic gesture! Almost *guaranteed* to get your face slapped.

466

And if you *really* want to get her steamed, suggest that the two of you make your very own home-made X-Rated video!

467

Compare her with this month's Playmate.

468

Compare her with the Victoria's Secret models.

469

Compare her with the *Sports Illustrated* swimsuit models. This is *especially* unromantic because the swimsuit issue comes out in *mid-February*—just when the average American woman is chunky and out of shape following the holidays, and in rather low spirits anyway.

Inappropriate Gifts

470

Here's a birthday gift sure to be talked about for years to come: A life-size cardboard stand-up of President Clinton. Only $24.98! From the *Funny Side Up* catalog: Call 215-361-5130; or write 425 Stump Rd., P.O. Box 2800, North Wales, PA 19454.

Reprinted with permission of United Feature Syndicate, Inc., Drabble © 1992

471

A collection of some of the least romantic gift items imaginable, including: An "intelligent" yo-yo; physics cartoon books; holograms; and plasma spheres. From the nerd's own MIT Museum Shop catalog. Call 617-253-4462, or write to 265 Massachusetts Ave., Cambridge, MA 03139.

472-477

More unromantic gifts:

- ✳ The "Buns of Steel" exercise tape
- ✳ Rakes
- ✳ A new set of steel-belted radials
- ✳ Godiva chocolates (when she's on a diet)
- ✳ A lifetime subscription to *TV Guide*
- ✳ Tickets to the Indianapolis 500

478

If you think she might be *offended* by a membership in the Panty-of-the-Month Club (Call 718-PANTIES), stick with something more conservative, yet still unromantic. I recommend that Potato-of-the-Month Club. Your lover will be delighted to receive "certified organically-grown potatoes in many of the old-fashioned, flavorful varieties—delivered to her door each month." For a free catalog write: P.O. Box 448-Y, Presque Isle, ME 04769; or call 800-827-7551.

479

Peek-a-boo bras and crotchless panties.

Ins & Outs

480

* Romantics have *friends*.
* Unromantics have *buddies*.

481

* Romantics have "loving wives."
* Unromantics have "My Old Lady"

482

* Romantics have "love gifts" hidden around the house for their wives.
* Unromantics have two-pound bags of M&M's hidden behind the couch for when their wives put them on a diet.

483

Even though smoking is a great unromantic habit, one paradoxical unromantic strategy that few people think of is to *stop smoking*. Why? Because nothing is more obnoxious than an ex-smoker! The first stage is that they're unbearably grouchy. In the second stage they gain 10 to 30 pounds of excess, unromantic fat. And in the final stage they become obnoxiously, proudly evangelistic about the fact that they quit smoking.

484

See above, regarding *drinking*.

485

Poet's Corner

Writing poetry is a sure way to a woman's heart. (And from there, into her *bedroom*.) So, here's some help for you guys who can't get past "Roses are red, violets are blue . . ." The tough part, you see, is coming up with appropriate words that rhyme with "blue" and "I love you." Here's a list to help you:

> *Igloo*
> *Screw*
> *Fondue*
> *Zoo*
> *Pew*
> *Brew*
> *Overdue*
> *Adieu*
> *Slew*
> *Coup*
> *Sue*
> *Achoo*
> *Chew*
> *Flu*
> *Gnu*

486

> "There is hardly any activity, any enterprise, which is started with such tremendous hopes and expectations and yet fails so regularly as love."
> ~ Erich Fromm

Isn't That Special?!

487-488

* The *most* romantic state in the United States of America? Hawaii, of course. What do you expect from a bunch of people who wear grass skirts, and who use one word—"*Aloha*"—for "Hello," "Goodbye," and "I love you." Seems very confusing to me!

* The *least* romantic state in the U.S. of A? Alaska, of course. There ain't many women there to begin with. It's not an environment well suited to maintaining nicely manicured fingernails. It's an environment better suited to lumberjacks, oil riggers, hunters and trappers. A manly paradise!

489-490

"But what about the *continental* U.S.?" you ask. Well, *okay*.

* My extensive research reveals that California and Vermont are tied for the dubious distinction of being the most romantic states.
* The least romantic state in the Union is North Dakota—followed closely by Wyoming, New Mexico, South Dakota and Oklahoma.

ISN'T THAT SPECIAL?!

491

Looking for a good way to waste some money on a stupid gift? Well, then, get a copy of the Eclectic American Catalog Company's "House of Windsor Collection." It's full of royal knickknacks and trinkets made by companies that make things for the British royal family. The venture is headed by Queen Elizabeth II's cousin Prince Michael of Kent. You, too can own chocolate Big Bens, mugs with the Queen's mug on them, and cheap neckties with pictures of Prince Charles on them.

492

An unromantic gift strategy: Give her *cash*—and tell her to buy her *own* present.

493

Nude beaches and nudist camps are great places for taking the romance, the mystery and the excitement out of seeing the bodies of members of the opposite sex. Send now for your copy of *The World Guide to Nude Beaches and Recreation*. Send $24.95 to The Naturist Society, P.O. Box 132, Oskosh, WI 54902.

494

Not all love letters are romantic . . . This quote is from a letter by George Bernard Shaw to Mrs. Patrick Campbell:

"I hope you have lost your good looks for while they last any fool can adore you, and the adoration of fools is bad for the soul. No, give me a ruined complexion and a lost figure and sixteen chins on a farmyard of crow's feet and an obvious wig. Then you shall see me come out strong."

It's a Mad, Mad, Mad, Mad World

495

German psychologist Niels Birbaumer, at Tuebingen University, has discovered that love makes you stupid! No lie! Using an electroencephalogram to measure the electrical activity of the brain, he has determined that when a person is engaged in high-level thinking, his brain waves are identifiably complex. But when people who were "genuinely, passionately in love" were tested, they exhibited brain wave patterns that were much simpler. Birbaumer's conclusion is that "Love makes you stupid." (This item was reported September 1, 1993, by the *London Observer Service*.) I think the lesson is obvious . . . in addition to all of the other reasons not to be romantic, we now have proof that love makes you dumb! [And I don't know about *you*, but I think there's already *plenty* of dumbness in the world!]

496

We are a nation of fools and babies. You want *proof*? A while back, some idiot wrote to *Ann Landers*, complaining that men never put the toilet seat down. Not only did this begin the "Great Toilet Seat Debate," it generated a flood of more than 20,000 letters to Ann Landers on the topic. *Think* about that for a moment: 20,000 adult Americans sat down and wrote letters about *toilet seats*. These same people probably never write love notes to their own spouses. Go figure!

497

Perhaps I shouldn't be so hard on Americans. People from around the world do some pretty inane things, too. Take this, for example: Some people actually write letters asking for advice from Juliet. You remember Juliet: She's a *fictional* character in Shakespeare's *Romeo and Juliet*. Not only that—she's a *dead* fictional character... and people *still* write to her! Now, here's the killer (no pun intended): Guess how many letters are sent to her. Go ahead, just *guess*. (Answer appears later in this item.)

People write to Juliet in Verona, Italy, where the story took place (in the 13th Century). And the letters are answered! Yes! There's actually something called the Club of Juliet that has volunteers who sit down and write back to the lovelorn from around the world! So, if you, too, have a pressing relationship problem, write to Juliet, Club di Giulietta, Stradone Maffei 2/b, Dept. P, 37121 Verona, Italy.

(Answer: 5,200 letters per year! That's about 100 letters per *week*! It *truly* is a mad, mad, mad, mad world!)

498-507

My survey of countries and cultures reveals some obvious winners and losers, and a few surprises!

Most Romantic Countries	Least Romantic Countries
Italy	USA
France	USA
Australia	Japan
Spain	USA
Brazil	Iran
Jamaica	Honduras
Thailand	Saudi Arabia
Argentina	Greenland
New Zealand	China
Morocco	India

508

New Orleans is touted as America's Most Romantic City, what with its French influence, the many jazz clubs, and of course, Mardi Gras. Maybe it's just me, but I fail to find the romance in a week-long drunken party, the main sport of which involves convincing young women to bare their breasts in exchange for a string of cheap plastic beads.

509

"The ironic side effect of women having abandoned their privileged status as 'ladies' is that they are now in danger of being as revolting as men, and accordingly treated, by men, as nothing special."
~ Quentin Crisp

It's All in Your Mind

510-512

How to *sound* romantic (when you're really *not*):
- ♠ "I'm taking my wife to the *islands* this winter." (The Falklands.)
- ♠ "Yeah, I bought her a *rock* for our anniversary." (A *pet* rock.)
- ♠ "We spend time reading together every day." (He reads the Sports Page while she reads the News over breakfast.)

513

"Women have more imagination than men. They need it to tell us how wonderful we are."
~ Arnold H. Glasgow

514

The battle of the sexes is the Natural Order of Things. To try to stop it, slow it, or divert is as foolish as trying to stop the tides.

515-520

Ways to ruin the mood:
- ☐ Immediately after making love, give him a detailed critique of his technique.
- ☐ Make your first kiss with her a *deep* French Kiss.
- ☐ While making love for the first time, say to him, "I love babies—don't you?!"
- ☐ Fall asleep immediately after sex.
- ☐ Keep the TV on during sex—so you can "catch the final scores."
- ☐ Call her by an ex-girlfriend's name at the height of passion.

Jerks R Us

521

A Holiday treat for you and your honey: The "Mistletoe Belt"—with mistletoe attached to the belt buckle. (Think about it.) Only $5.98. From the *Funny Side Up* catalog: Call 215-361-5130; or write 425 Stump Rd., P.O. Box 2800, North Wales, PA 19454.

522

Not romantic: "Beavis and Butt-Head." *Heh-heh. Heh-heh. Heh-heh. Heh-heh. Heh-heh. Heh-heh. Heh-heh.*

♦ JERKS R US ♦

523

I'm simply going to reprint this article from the *Orange County Register* without making any editorial comments:

"You promise to love, honor and obey—but not necessarily to shower, shave and get a job. Donald Johnston, 55, was appalled to see his marriage annulled last year by a Santa Ana judge who ruled that Johnston had defrauded his bride by turning into a slob after they got married.

The finding allowed Brenda Joyce Johnston to take sole possession of the couple's Anaheim home. But this week, an appeals court ruled that having unexpectedly shoddy bathroom habits is not grounds for an annulment and a finding of fraud. Justices of the 4th District Court of Appeals granted Donald Johnston a divorce instead, throwing out the fraud ruling and rendering a house held jointly by the couple into community property.

They said deceit or a false assertion made before the marriage is necessary to prove fraud. Donald P. Bebereia, Donald Johnston's lawyer, said: 'He never promised her he would take a shower'."

524-527

We all know that cruises are Hell. Here are some variations of Hell that have been devised by those devils in the travel industry:

✔ **Round-the-World Cruises**: 98 solid days of vomiting.

✔ **Sports Cruises**: You get to travel in cramped quarters with retired football and basketball stars. Mmmm, fun!

✔ **Canal Cruises**: Tedious, yet boring and slow barges take you through the European countryside. I've always wanted to cruise on a *barge*. Yeah, *right*!

✔ **Antarctic Adventure Cruises**: Instead of staying home all winter and freezing your ass off, you can now pay lots of money to do the same thing on a *boat*. Imagine the thrill of experiencing seasickness in 40° below zero weather, heaving your guts out while clutching the icy railing of the ship, as the quaint and picturesque penguins laugh at you.

528

While out on a date, flirt with other women: Her friends, waitresses, stewardesses, etc. (She'll pretend to be angry, but she'll secretly be proud to know that you're aggressive and virile.)

Lessons from Nerds

529

Vying for the Number 1 spot among unromantics are the *engineers* of the world. Why? They've turned logic into a kind-of *religion*. They understand the workings of the atom, but are clueless about the workings of the human heart. Engineers *define* the meaning of the phrase "anal-retentive." They view the world in black and white.

And although most engineers are men, a few women have infiltrated the ranks. From Ann Landers' column: "My wife is an engineer. She is precise, analytical and definite in her views, and she always thinks before she speaks. She's as cold as ice and so sure of herself she makes me sick. My next wife will probably be an empty-headed, bubbly moron and it will be a relief."

530-534

Unromantic accessories for men:
- Plastic pocket protectors
- Thick bifocals
- Clodhopper shoes
- I.D. bracelets
- Black ankle sox

❦ LESSONS FROM NERDS ❦

535

How to keep a nerd happy for hours . . . or days . . . or weeks: *The Joy of Mathematics*, by Theoni Pappas. "mathematics is a science, a language, an art, a way of thinking. It appears in nature, art, music, architecture, literature. This unforgettable and immensely popular book reveals the influence of mathematics in our everyday lives. [Oh, *boy*!] The book also offers a selection of entertaining exercises." Only $10.95

536

How to keep a nerd happy after he's done with *The Joy of Mathematics* . . . you get him *More Joy of Mathematics*, of course! *This* edition is filled with ideas, puzzles and games from around the world.

537

For sports nuts who are *also* nerds: *The Physics of Baseball*, by Robert K. Adair. This book unfolds all the physics and formulae of baseball with vivid examples from pro-ball play. Learn the dynamics of the curve ball, the knuckle ball, and the hop of a fast ball. Only $9 from the MIT Museum Shop at 617-253-4462.

538

For nerds with a sense of humor: *The Cartoon Guide to Physics*, by Larry Gonick & Art Huffman. With the help of these cartoons you won't need to be an Einstein to understand the concepts of velocity, acceleration, gravity, electricity, magnetism, and even quantum electrodynamics. Only $10 from the MIT Museum Shop at 617-253-4462.

539

Use black electrical tape to fix your broken glasses.

Lessons from the Bible

540

"Love thy neighbor as thyself." ~ The Bible
"But don't let your wife catch you." ~ Joe Magadatz

541

"What woman wants, God also wants."
~ Old French proverb

542

*"In sorrow shalt thou bring forth children;
and thy desire shall be to thy husband,
and he shall rule over thee."*
~ God to Eve

543

"The first time Adam had a chance, he laid the blame on women."
~ Nancy Astor

544

*"God made man, and then said I can do better than that
and made woman."*
~ Adela Rogers St. John

Lessons from The 3 Stooges

545

Phrases that don't seem to impress women:

Nyuk-nyuk-nyuk!
Oh—a wise guy!
Whoo-woo-woo-woo-woo-woo!
You knucklehead!

546

For the stooge in your love life: The *Three Stooges Calendar*! Only $10.95! From the *Funny Side Up* catalog: Call 215-361-5130; or write 425 Stump Rd., P.O. Box 2800, North Wales, PA 19454.

547

➢ Romantics know all the words to *You Light Up My Life*.
➢ Unromantics know all 99 verses of *99 Bottles of Beer on the Wall*.

548

✱ Romantics can quote from *The Bridges of Madison County* in moments of passion.
✱ Unromantics can quote from *Truly Tasteless Jokes* (Volumes I *and* II) at the most inopportune moments.

549

I know that this one *goes without saying* . . . but I need just *one more* item to make this book come out to exactly 1001 items, so . . . Men, don't forget, it's against our Code of Guy Ethics to stop and ask for directions, even when—*especially* when—you're hopelessly lost.

550

Watch *The Three Stooges* every Saturday morning on TV. Better yet! Record them on video, so you can enjoy them *anytime*! (Don't forget, even with ESPN, there is *not* a live sports game being telecast during every moment of every day. What are you supposed to do during the in-between times? —Why, watch *The Three Stooges*, of course!

Life Is a Cabaret

551-557

A week of unromance . . .

Sunday—Don't shave all weekend. Lounge in your underwear. Watch sports on TV.

Monday—Back to work. *Bleech!*

Tuesday—Work late.

Wednesday—Hump Day.

Thursday—Poker Nite.

Friday—TGIF. Happy Hour after work. Don't return home until after 2 a.m.

Saturday—"Hangover Day." Watch cartoons in the morning, sports in the afternoon.

558

Guys: Talk about things that she has *absolutely no interest in*: The Knicks; golf; carburetors; the latest screen-saver on your computer; golf; Star Trek; your stock investments; golf.

559

Gals: Chatter on about things that he has *absolutely no interest in*: Your job; your hair; your friends; your likes and dislikes; your wishes and dreams. —Actually, anything except sex will probably put him right to sleep.

560

"Marriage is an alliance entered into by a man who can't sleep with the window shut, and a woman who can't sleep with the window open."
~ George Bernard Shaw

Losers & Weiners

561-567

More unromantic role models:

- Homer Simpson
- Al Bundy
- HAL, from *2001: A Space Odyssey*
- Dave Barry
- Stephen King
- Pee Wee Herman
- Archie Bunker

◆ LOSERS & WEINERS ◆

568

*"A man in love is incomplete until he is married.
Then he is finished."*
~ Zsa Zsa Gabor

569

Republicans are more unromantic than Democrats.

570

Conservatives are more unromantic than Liberals.

571

Podiatrists are more unromantic than Orthodontists.

572

Methodists and Episcopalians are more unromantic than Baptists and Catholics.

573

The East Coast is more unromantic than the West Coast.

574

The North is more unromantic than the South.

Love Is A Many Splintered Thing

575

"Love is like an hourglass, with the heart filling up as the brain empties."
~ Jules Renard

576

*"No woman ever falls in love with a man unless
she has a better opinion of him
than he deserves."*
~ Ed Howe

Reprinted with permission of NEA, Inc., The Born Loser © 1993

577

*"Love is constant, it is we who are fickle.
Love does guarantee, people betray.
Love can always be trusted, people cannot."*
~ Leo Buscaglia

[Is this supposed to be inspiring or *depressing*??]

✤ LOVE IS BLIND ✤

578

"Love is the triumph of imagination over intelligence."
~ H.L. Mencken

579

"Love is the self-delusion we manufacture to justify the trouble we take to have sex."
~ Dan Greenburg

Love Is Blind

580

What is the deal with Love, anyway? We get burned again and again, and yet we keep coming back for more—like a moth attracted to a deadly, burning flame. There must be a masochistic gene in us somewhere.

581

"Love is the answer, but while you're waiting for the answer, sex raises some pretty good questions."
~ Woody Allen

Male Bashing

582

"The more I see of men, the more I like dogs."
~ Madame de Stael

✦ MALE BASHING ✦

583

How many men does it take to change a lightbulb? —None! They all know if they wait long enough, a woman will do it. Why are all "dumb blonde" jokes one-liners? —So men can understand them.

The *Dumb Men Jokes* book will keep your friends laughing . . . and your man either steamed or confused. Only $3.98! From the *Funny Side Up* catalog: Call 215-361-5130; or write 425 Stump Rd., P.O. Box 2800, North Wales, PA 19454.

584

"Some of us are becoming the men we wanted to marry."
~ Gloria Steinem

585

"I married beneath me—all women do."
~ Nancy Astor

586

"Most men do not mature, they simply grow taller."
~ Leo Rosten

587-588

Men (attempts to define):

"Unusually low voices; short life expectancies; odd, drab costumes; a tendency to sweat, fart and yell."
~ C.E. Crimmins

"The male is a domestic animal which, if treated with firmness and kindness, can be trained to do most things."
~ Jilly Cooper

Mama Mia!

589

(From *USA Today*) "More women than men say wives should stay home and husbands should work, a new Gallup poll shows. Many of the findings in the nationwide poll of 1,065 adults, conducted for USA Today and CNN, will not gladden the hearts of feminists: 45% of women say it is better for society if "the man is the achiever outside the home, and the woman takes care of home and family;" 40% of men agree . . . 48% of women think the women's movement has made women's lives harder than 20 years ago . . . Katherine Spillar of the Feminist Majority says the poll simply shows women are upset and frustrated." So what *else* is new?!

590

Romantic turn-offs: Cross-dressing.

591

Romantic turn-offs: B.O.

592

Romantic turn-offs (for women): Season tickets—even if they *are* on the 50-yard line!

593

Romantic turn-offs (for men): Season tickets—to the *opera* . . . no matter *where* in the theatre they are.

594

Widening the gap between men and women: In college, while the frat guys are getting blitzed on beer and planning the next Toga party—the sorority girls are making party favors and planning the next formal ball. Is it any *wonder* men and women don't communicate?!

Men vs. Women

595

Women hate being called . . . "My Old Lady" . . . "The Little Woman" . . . "My Cellulite Cutie."

596

Men hate being called . . . late for dinner.

597

Blame all of her bad moods on PMS.

Mindset of an Unromantic

598

I long for the "old" Tim Allen, who would hoot like a monkey and state his manly philosophy unapologetically and hysterically! The "new" Tim Allen, of recent *Home Improvement* fame, is getting increasingly watered-down. A message to the writers and producers: It's getting tiring to have him learn a lesson in sensitivity in every episode. *Aaar-aaar!*

599

Unromantics prefer Frederick's of Hollywood to Victoria's Secret.

600

Unromantics prefer Holiday Inns to the Four Seasons.

601

Unromantics prefer pick-up trucks to sports cars.

602

Unromantics prefer IBMs to Macintoshes.

603

Unromantics prefer steak to swordfish.

604

Unromantics prefer dogs to cats. Big dogs. Mean dogs.

Miscommunicating for Fun & Profit

605

One great way to reduce the amount of communication in your life is to wear a Walkman.

606

Some couples manage to be "together" and "apart" at the same time. I've actually seen couples walking down the street, hand-in-hand, each wearing a separate Walkman. I just can't figure out if they're being romantically unromantic, or unromantically romantic.

Reprinted with permission of United Feature Syndicate, Inc., Guy Stuff © 1993

607-610

Least romantic phrases:

- "You eediot!"
- "I love you—*not!*"
- "Well, *excuuuuse me!*"
- "Today is the first day of the rest of your life."

611-613

A few more unromantic phrases:

- "Happy happy, joy joy!"
- "Yabba dabba doo!" (Especially during sex.)
- "Have a nice day."

614-620

As a public service, here are a few selections from the *Gender Translation Dictionary*:

- **She says**: "How about a little romance?"
- **She means**: "Let's go out for dinner and a little dancing."

- **He says**: "How about a little romance?"
- **He means**: "Let's have sex."

- **She says**: "You can take my car if you like."
- **She means**: "My car needs gas."

- **He says**: "I've had a tough week. I'm really beat."
- **He means**: "Will you give me a back rub?"

- **She says**: "I've had a tough week, too!"
- **She means**: "No way, Jose!"

- **He says**: "It's been ages since we've spent time alone together."
- **He means**: "It's been ages since we've had sex."

- **She says**: "It's been ages since we've spent time alone together."
- **She means**: "It's been ages since we've had a heart-to-heart *talk*."

621

Roll your eyes when she's talking to you... then deny that you did it. ("It was just a *twitch*! An uncontrollable physical spasm! I may have a serious medical problem here and you just want to *criticize* me!" —Then storm out of the room.)

622

Turn every intimate discussion into an argument.

Money Can't Buy You Love

623

*"I don't think I'll get married again.
I'll just find a woman I don't like and give her a house."*
~ Lewis Grizzard

624

Retail stores that are *never* visited by unromantics: Crabtree & Evelyn; Victoria's Secret; florist shops; Hallmark card shops; any store referred-to as a "boutique"; any shop that smells like *potpourri*; any shop with "Whimsical" in its title.

625

If you equate dollars-spent with love-expressed, then you'll *love* this little package that Hotel Nikko Chicago, along with Tiffany & Company, have put together. The "Engagement Package," for only $29,000 gives you all this: A two-carat diamond engagement ring; a jazz duo playing your favorite songs while you dine in the Presidential Suite; roses; a private butler; monogrammed bathrobes; and a carriage ride. For more information, call the Hotel Nikko Chicago at 312-744-1900.

626

"If women didn't exist, all the money in the world would have no meaning."
~ Aristotle Onassis

Monotony—Not Monogamy

627

"If there is such a thing as Platonic love between a man and a woman, it is the result of some profound misunderstanding, a stifling of their true and authentic impulses."
~ Ivan Mestrovic

628

They say that reading aloud to each other is romantic. I *tried* this with my first wife. It didn't work. We got divorced in the middle of Volume M-N of the *Encyclopedia Britannica*.

Not being one to give up easily, I attempted reading *War and Peace* aloud to my second wife. Needless to say, we got divorced before we ever got to *peace*.

629

"Getting married, like getting hanged, is a great deal less dreadful than it has been made out."
~ H.L. Mencken

More Bad Habits

630

Spitting. *Truly* an unromantic habit. [Social scientists used to believe that spitting was culturally conditioned. But biologists have recently identified what they are tentatively calling the "Spitting Gene" on the male chromosome. Stay tuned for further developments.]

631

Be suspicious. Open her mail. Listen-in to her phone conversations. (She'll pretend to be irritated, but secretly she's glad to know that you care.)

632

Finish her sentences for her. Tell the punchlines of the jokes she's relating. Tell her what she's thinking. (She'll pretend to resent all of these things, but she'll secretly appreciate you for knowing her so well.)

633

Chewing tobacco. Unromantic, unhealthy and disgusting—all at the same time!

Most Illogical

634

Oxymorons:

Military intelligence
Jumbo shrimp
Romantic men

635

Here's a paradox for you: The traits that attract people to one another are often the very things that cause break-ups! A survey taken at the University of California, as reported in *Glamour Magazine*, illustrated this phenomenon:

What women like about men—that later became a turn-off

Attracting traits	turned into	*Detracting traits*
Funny and fun		Embarrassed me in public
Spontaneous		Irresponsible
Relaxed		Constantly late
Confident		Acted like a god
Successful and focused		Workaholic
Strong willed		Macho

What men like about women—that later became a turnoff

Attracting traits	turned into	*Detracting traits*
Nurturing		Smothering
Intense interest in me		Jealous and possessive
Offbeat personality		Too unconventional
Strong		Domineering
Willing to have sex		Always wanted sex

636

Theatre Review of Allegedly Romantic Shows
Phantom of the Opera

Women swoon over this show. Here's the story: Boy meets girl. Boy tutors girl in opera. Girl removes boy's mask revealing The Worst Case of Acne You've Ever Seen. Love Triangle ensues. Boy hurls chandelier onto stage in a fit of rage. Boy writes truly atrocious opera. Various murders throughout. Girl sings. Boy kidnaps girl. Lets her go. The end.
The lesson? Take heart, oh ye of Clearasil addiction—there's hope for you yet.

637

If your idea of a romantic time is gambling your money away, then by all means, take a vacation in Las Vegas. Better yet, why don't you save yourself the airfare and the hassles, and just pile several thousand dollars in small bills in your fireplace and set them aflame?

638

"Most hierarchies were established by men who now monopolize the upper levels, thus depriving women of their rightful share of opportunities for incompetence."
~ Laurence Peter

Movie Madness

639

Movie Review of Allegedly Romantic Classics
West Side Story

Boy meets girl. Boy kills girl's brother. Brother's friends kill boy. The end. (Note: Blatant rip-off of Shakespeare's *Romeo and Juliet*.)

640

Movie Review of Allegedly Romantic Classics
Gone With the Wind

Soldier meets southern belle. Belle makes dress out of drapes. Something about a war. Plantation burns. Soldier tells belle he doesn't give a damn. [*Why* do women love this movie?!]

641

Movie Reviews of Allegedly Romantic Classics
True Romance

With a title like this, how could you miss? Here's how: Boy meets girl. They somehow get a suitcase full of cocaine. Cops and Mafia chase them across the country. People murdered left and right—but it's *still* romantic (so they say). Maybe it's *me*. I just don't see the romance in all of this. Here's what the *New York Times* has to say: "The body count is sprinkled like confetti through 'True Romance,' as cops shoot it out with mobsters, someone's head is bashed in . . . Yet it would be wrongheaded to get worked up over the apparent amorality or violence in the hot genre picture of the moment. This is a tale of young lovers . . . who accidentally fall into murderous doings and still manage to remain sweet kids." I guess if my kids ever murder someone, I'll simply tell the cops that they're being "wrongheaded" about the whole thing.

642

I've never viewed Clint Eastwood as a romantic hero, but perhaps I'm wrong. In reviewing the highly-violent/typically Eastwood thriller *In the Line of Fire*, the Hollywood Radio Syndicate said, "Eastwood hits the bullseye: he is larger than life, tougher than nails and irresistibly romantic . . . in this classic nail-biting thriller."

643-652

Top 10 Least Romantic Movies:

1. *Alien*
2. *Silence of the Lambs*
3. *Animal House*
4. *Rocky Horror Picture Show*
5. *Buckaroo Bonsai*
6. *Love Story*
7. *The Day the Earth Stood Still*
8. *Rocky IV*
9. *Reefer Madness*
10. *Boxing Helena*

Music & Other Mush

653-665

Favorite Unromantic Songs

Why Don't We Do It In the Road
The Streak
The Masochism Tango
Disco Duck
I'm A Girl-Watcher
The Wreck of the Edmund Fitzgerald
I Got You, Babe
A Horse With No Name
In Heaven There Is No Beer (That's Why We Drink It Here)
Stayin' Alive
Short People
I'm Just a Gigolo

♦ MUSIC & OTHER MUSH ♦

666-671

Allegedly Romantic Songs That Make Most People Retch

Having My Baby
Muskrat Love
You Light Up My Life
Forever In Blue Jeans
How Deep Is Your Love?
Sunshine (On My Shoulder)

672

Yodeling is *not* romantic.

673-675

Some of the most unromantic songs of all time, as compiled by Dr. Demento:

- *A Bowl of Chop Suey and You-ey*, by Sam Robbins & His Hotel McAlpin Orchestra
- *I've Got Tears in My Ears from Lying on My Back in Bed While I Cry Over You*, by Homer & Jethro
- *How Could You Believe Me When I Said I Loved You When You Know I've Been a Liar All My Life*, by Fred Astaire & Jane Powell

676

Rock 'n Roll music signaled the end or romantic "close dancing." Dancing to rock is an exercise in self-expression, or maybe it's just plain exercise. Anyway—anything that leads to the Funky Chicken and Slam Dancing can't be all bad, eh?

♦ COWABUNGA! ♦

Mutant Teenage Ninja Turtles

677

The military is one of the last bastions of the truly practical, no-nonsense, unromantic lifestyle. What a glorious approach to life! Everything is neatly black and white, "Yes, sir!" and "No, sir!" It's logically hierarchical. And it is (or *was*) all male.

678

It's not that we unromantics are *paranoid* . . . but a lot of people *do* seem to be out to get us: whiny women; male apologists; the PC Brigade (those oh-so Politically Correct folks); "sensitive guys"; the wedding industry; TV talk show hosts; and—not that I want to single-out anybody in particular, *but*—Leo Buscaglia, John Bradshaw, and Gregory J.P. Godek [Where does this guy get off using two middle initials, anyway?!]

679-683

More unromantic role models:
- Woody Allen
- Woody Woodpecker
- Larry "Bud" Melman
- Spuds MacKenzie
- Steven Jobs

684

"The whole world is strewn with snares, traps, gins, and pitfalls for the capture of men by women."
~ George Bernard Shaw

Nagging & Other Techniques

685

Nagging. Guys, you could learn a lot from women about this excellent unromantic strategy. Take notes... Basic, generic nagging is fine, but the accomplished unromantic will want to add a variety of nagging techniques to their repertoire:

- The Public Nag
- The Slam-Dunk Nag
- The Whiney Nag
- The Arrogant Nag
- The All-Purpose Roseanne Nag
- The Piggish Miss Piggy Nag
- The Shrill Nag
- The Guilt-Producing Nag
- The Anger-Producing Nag
- The Out-of-the-Blue Nag
- The Back-Seat Nag

686-690

Unromantic names to call your wife or girlfriend:

Hey, You
Strumpet
Jiggle Queen
C.T.
Mommy

691-697

Unromantic things to call your husband or boyfriend:

- Pee Wee
- Love Muffin
- Meal Ticket
- Fartmeister
- Baldy
- Butt-Head
- Pencil-Necked Geek

698-702

One of the greatest unromantic strategies in the book is *The Double-Standard*. Apply it often and creatively!

- Show up half an hour late for dates . . . and then lecture her about being irresponsible the first time *she's* late.
- Toss your underwear on the bedroom floor . . . and then accuse *her* of being a sloppy housecleaner.
- Dress like a slob . . . and then criticize her for not being fashionable.
- Tell him he's a sexist pig because he thinks Kim Basinger is hot in *Nine-1/2 Weeks* . . . and then swoon over Mel Gibson in *Lethal Weapon*.
- Ask repeatedly . . . "Where are my car keys?"—"Where's my wallet?"—"Where are my clean sox?"—"Where's the TV remote control?" . . . and then criticize *her* for being unorganized.

703-704

More effective unromantic communication techniques:

- **For him**: Sulk—don't talk—when you're mad.
- **For her**: Pout—don't talk—when you're mad.

- **For him**: Go out and get drunk after your most recent fight.
- **For her**: Tell your girlfriends every intimate detail of your most recent fight.

705

Another favorite unromantic strategy: *Offer unsolicited advice.* About her driving... about balancing his checkbook... about her weight... about his spending habits... about her wardrobe... about his eating habits.

Nice Guys Finish Last

706

Nice Guys Finish Last... It's not just a clever *chapter* title—it's a *book* title! Author Marcus Pierce Meleton, Jr. takes a light hearted approach to the burning question "Why are so many women attracted to the jerks of the world?" If you're too embarrassed to ask for it at your local bookstore, call the publisher at 714-645-0139; or write to Sharkbait Press, P.O. Box 11300, Costa Mesa, CA 92627. Only $7.95!

707

A recent member of the Unromantics' Hall of Fame: Howard Stern. (Of course, there's a fine line between being an unromantic and being an asshole—and Howard swings both ways.)

708

[Marriage is] "... far and away the most sanitary and least harmful of all the impossible forms of the man-woman relationship, though I would sooner jump off the Brooklyn Bridge than be married."
~ H.L. Mencken

709

Book Review of Allegedly Romantic Classics
The Bridges of Madison County

Enigmatic photographer travels cross-country to shoot some damn bridges. Meets lonely housewife. Brief affair ensues. ("She, who had ceased having orgasms years ago, had them in long sequences now with a half-man, half-something-else creature. She wondered about him and his endurance, and he told her that he could reach those places in his mind as well as physically, and that the orgasms of the mind had their own special character." *Uh-huh.*) They discover a True and Deep and Passionate Love That Comes Along Only Once In a Millennium. So what do they do about this Cosmic Discovery? Nothing! He leaves, and lives the rest of his life a lonely man. She passes the years quietly (but writes it all down, so her grown kids can discover it later). The moral of the story? *Nice Guys Finish Last.*

710

Keep "His" and "Hers" overnight bags in your car trunk for those "Surprise Escape Weekends." Packing tips:

* **His bag**: A six-pack; condoms; beer nuts; clean underwear.
* **Her bag**: Lingerie.

711

Guys, read the book *You Just Don't Understand*, by Deborah Tannen. It will help you learn how to pretend to listen to her.

712

Gals, read the book *Iron John*, by Robert Bly. It will give you a chuckle.

Norm!!

713

Let's now have a moment of silence to honor the patron saint of beer-drinkers everywhere, Norm Peterson. Quiet please . . . *burp!*

714

I searched the world over to find this out: The beer with the highest alcohol content. And the winner is . . . Samuel Adams Triple Bock. It has 17.4% alcohol (versus 4%-5% for regular beer).

715

And for those of you for whom *drinking* beer isn't enough—you'd like to *eat* it, too . . . there's the Great American Beer Cookbook. It includes recipes such as chocolate stout pie. Author/chef Candy Schermerhorn says, "When a recipe calls for water or milk, replace it with beer and powdered milk. It'll add great flavor." Only $24.95! Check your local bookstore or call 303-546-6514.

Oh, Shit!

716

- Every day more than 10,000 American men turn 40.
- The average American watches 6.75 hours of TV per day.

✦ OH, SHIT! ✦

717

Unromantic phrases (Category: "Sex")

- "You do that *almost* as well as my last boyfriend."
- "I though *you* took care of the birth control!"
- "Did you come yet?"
- "Is it in yet?"

718

Romantics with visions of Glenn Miller's Chattanooga Choo Choo will be disappointed to discover that the train's terminal has been converted into a Holiday Inn. But rest assured, the famous steam train still chugs along. While visiting beautiful Chattanooga, Tennessee, make sure you visit nearby Lynchburg, where you can tour the Jack Daniels Distillery.

719

I actually found a place that sells golf balls with "OH SHIT" printed on them. Only in America...! 3 for $7.98. From the *Funny Side Up* catalog: Call 215-361-5130; or write 425 Stump Rd., P.O. Box 2800, North Wales, PA 19454.

720

The Worst Advice Ever Given to a Young Man: "Be yourself." Be yourself? *Be yourself??!* Why would you want to be *yourself*? You're a *slob*! You're *insecure*! You're *poor*! —You don't want to be *yourself*! You want to be *Tom Selleck*! You want to be *Tom Cruise*! You want to be *Arnold Schwarzenegger*!

Playboy of the Western World

721

"It ain't bragging if you can do it."
~ Dizzy Dean

722

If you want to display the fact that you're a playboy—and frankly not interested in *commitment* or *communication*, but only a *good time*—you should invest in a wardrobe of outfits with the Playboy bunny logo on them. Polo shirts, T-shirts, caps, towels, jackets and underwear are all available from the *Playboy Catalog*. Call for a free catalog: 800-423-9494; or write *Playboy Catalog*, P.O. Box 809, Itasca, IL 60143.

723

Did you ever wonder where the phrase "In like Flynn" came from? It became a popular phrase in 1943 when Errol Flynn was tried (and acquitted) of statutory rape.

724

Another book for your Unromantics Library: *Iron Joe Bob*, by John Bloom. It's an outrageous send-up of Robert Bly's bestselling yet sappy *Iron John*, which began the so-called Men's Movement. Bloom is hard on us guys. He believes that modern men are weenies. "If you look at history, we started out as Conan the Barbarian and ended up as Ward Cleaver." His book identifies the top five partying schools in America, provides a guide to dating in the 90s, and explains why women are crazy, but men are crazier.

Real Men Aren't Romantic

725

It's a common misconception that you have to be *macho* in order to be unromantic. *Untrue!* Some of the most successful unromantics are nerds, wimps and/or couch potatoes.

726

Don't get me *wrong*—having a macho mindset is a great *help* in being an unromantic, but it doesn't *automatically* make you an unromantic. You see, the macho philosophy of male dominance does allow for flowers and candy and bullshit like that.

727-732

Other personality types that make great unromantics are:

☆ Guys who think they're "God's Gift to Women"
☆ Militant feminists
☆ Workaholics
☆ Lawyers and accountants (But that goes without saying, doesn't it?!)
☆ Golfers
☆ Telephone repairmen

733

Some additions for *Roget's Thesaurus*: Synonyms for "romantic" as an adjective: Henpecked; pussy-whipped; wimp-o-rama; Mr. Mom; Hallmark-aholic; Donahue-esque.

734

Unromantics know the secrets of staying busy—some would say *obsessed*—with hobbies and projects. Here's a valuable resource for your Unromantics Library: *The Best Kits Catalog: Top-of-the-Line, Time-Tested Kits for Constructing Practically Anything*, by Frank Coffee. These projects could keep you occupied and distracted for two *lifetimes*! Everything from hooked rugs to rocking horses, from classic cars to aircraft! Only $15 from the MIT Museum Shop catalog. Call 617-253-4462, or write to 265 Massachusetts Ave., Cambridge, MA 03139.

Real *Women* Aren't Romantic

735

Further evidence that you needn't be *macho* in order to be unromantic: Women can be unromantic, too! Yes—unromance is an equal opportunity concept. So go for it ladies! First you got the vote, then you got to smoke cigarettes, then you got to fight in wars—and now you can be unromantic, too! It's a glorious world, ain't it?!

736

"Hell hath no fury like a woman scorned."
~ William Congreve

737

Least Romantic Profession for a Woman: Roller Derby.

◆ REAL WOMEN AREN'T ROMANTIC ◆

738

Women used to be more romantic than men. But the gap is closing. Women are becoming less romantic all the time. Women's Liberation is largely, but not entirely, responsible. Our changing cultural role models are having an effect, too. Girls in the 50s and 60s had the Barbie Doll as a role model. Girls in the 70s had Miss Piggy. Girls in the 80s had Roseanne Arnold. [I'm all for unromance—but in this case, perhaps the pendulum has swung *too far*!]

Reprinted with permission of Tribune Media Services, Inc., Suburban Cowgirls © 1993

739

Ladies: You can be practical and unromantic all at the same time simply by wearing a flannel nightgown to bed. It will keep you warm and discourage your amorous partner at the same time! (You get Bonus Points for wearing socks to bed, completing the outfit.)

Reality 101

740

"Love is a grave mental disease."
~ Plato

741

If you want to go on a really *unromantic* vacation, take a cruise! "What?!" you exclaim, "I thought cruises were *very* romantic!" Nay, nay! Consider these points, then we'll talk:

- Sea sickness
- Claustrophobic cabins
- Nightmares of the Titanic
- The healthy diet of only 23,000 calories per day
- Nightmares of *The Love Boat*

742

The most unromantic companies in America:

- General Motors
- IBM
- Proctor & Gamble
- AT&T
- 3M
- Marriott Corporation
- Merrill Lynch & Co.
- NYNEX
- Xerox

743

White water rafting: Fun, exhilarating, challenging?—Yes! Romantic?—Hell, *no!*

- Maine: Northern Outdoors: 800-765-7238
- California: Parks & Recreation Department: 916-988-0205
- West Virginia: Songer Whitewater: 800-356-RAFT
- Arizona: Grand Canyon National Park: 602-638-7843

744-747

More differences between men and women:

- Men lie about their height.
- Women lie about their weight.
- Men lie about their income.
- Women lie about their age.
- Men lie about the age when they lost their virginity. (They claim they were *younger*.)
- Women lie about the age when they lost their virginity. (They claim they were *older*.)
- Men lie about the number of sexual partners they've had.
- Women lie about their breast size.

748

Disney World, Revisited: I see nothing romantic about a six-foot rodent roaming the streets, hugging little children—and charging their parents a fortune for the privilege.

Revenge Is Sweet

749

Wake up, guys! Do you really think that the women's magazines are simply full of fluff? Here's a Classified Ad from *Cosmo*, reprinted verbatim: "Essential Publications for the 90s: *Divorce Dirty Tricks* (before, during or after divorce); *Complete Encyclopedia of Revenge Techniques*. $19.95 each, $34.95 both. B.H. Center, Inc., P.O. Box 5174, Richmond, KY 40476. Visa/MC (Instant Shipping!) 1-606-281-4614." *Yikes!*

Reprinted with permission of United Feature Syndicate, Inc., Garfield © 1993

750

A warning: Be careful not to get *too* zealous with your unromantic antics. There sometimes is a fine line between clever revenge and illegal nastiness. The following is from an Associated Press story: "SANTA ROSA, Calif. — A man who was steamed over his divorce admitted he sabotaged his ex-wife's computer files and was ordered to stand trial on a felony computer-tampering charge. James Welsh, 32, told authorities he sent a disk with a 'kamikaze program' to get back at his former wife, Kathleen Shelton, 51, for the nastiness of their 1991 divorce, said sheriff's Deputy Dennis Smiley.

Shelton testified that all her computer files were erased when she used the disk. All that was left was a taunting limerick, she said. The hacker hubby could face a maximum sentence of three years in prison if convicted."

751

"When a man steals your wife, there is no better revenge than to let him keep her."
~ Sacha Guitry

752

Another story from Associated Press: "QUESNEL, British Columbia — She locked him out of the house. So he tore it down with his bulldozer. Mildred Stychyshyn said her boyfriend, an unemployed bulldozer operator, was mad because she wouldn't let him in when he came home drunk. So he started up his bulldozer and smashed her wooden house to pieces, she said. "He told me that if he couldn't live in the house, neither could I," Stychyshyn said.

Police arrested 50-year-old Leon Roger Hetu Friday night after he leveled the house in Quesnel, 260 miles north of Vancouver, police Constable Paul Collister said. He told police he couldn't stand Stychyshyn's nagging any more, Collister said."

753

"When you consider what a chance women have to poison their husbands, it's a wonder there isn't more of it done."
~ Kin Hubbard

Run Like Hell

754

Romance defined

According to The Random House Dictionary, Second Edition Unabridged: Romantic: "Fanciful; impractical; unrealistic . . . imaginary, fictitious, or fabulous." Need I say more?

755-764

Top Ten Unromantic Topics of Conversation:

1. Particle physics
2. Your gall bladder operation
3. Your strange uncle Herbert
4. Explaining the meaning of *2001: A Space Odyssey*
5. Why your last lover's fellatio/cunnilingus technique was inadequate
6. The national debt
7. Golf
8. Your personal conspiracy theory of the assassination of JFK
9. Sports
10. Sports

765

Ladies, if you have some persistent Romeo pestering you and you want to get rid of him, simply utter three little letters—"PMS"—and you'll send him running for the hills.

766

"Wymyn." Have you seen this word yet? Well, be on the look-out for it. The radical feminists are at it again. *Wymyn* is their "Non-sexist" spelling of *woman*. Give me a break, gals. [Although I must say, it *is* unromantic. I can't imagine *any* guy wanting to be romantic—or even sexual, for that matter—with any *woman* who would spell it *wymyn*.]

767

Some observations:

Men: Men are superior to women. Well, we're stronger. And more logical—aren't we? . . . We're better drivers. And we're, uh, better at mathematics and mechanical abilities. Yeah! (Aren't we?) . . . Well, anyway, WE'RE **LOUDER!!**

Ladies: Just leave them alone, and they'll self-destruct.

♦ *"DAMMIT, JIM—I'M A DOCTOR, NOT A COMEDIAN!"* ♦

Science Fiction

768

For the high-tech unromantic: *Computer porn*! Yes, you can get software called *Virtual Photo Shoot* in which you can become a centerfold "photographer." You get to choose the physical characteristics of your model; you get to pose her; you get to zoom in on any part of her anatomy. *Yikes!*

769

There are also a variety of computer sex games and many erotic offerings via network. For an overview, you could pick-up a copy of *The Joy of Cybersex: An Undergound Guide to Electronic Erotica*, by Phillip Robinson and Nancy Tamosaitis.

770

The guy that women *least* want their man to emulate: RuPaul, the outrageous singer and transvestite phenomenon.

771

"Women's liberation is just a lot of foolishness.
It's men who are discriminated against. They can't bear children.
And no one's likely to do anything about that."
~ Golda Meir

772

Most Unromantic Music of All Time: *Anything/everything* by Yoko Ono.

Setting the Record Straight

773-777

It's untrue that unromantics don't feel love. We love . . .
. . . our dogs.
. . . our favorite football team.
. . . our favorite easy chair.
. . . our bookies.
. . . our TVs.

778-782

Contrary to popular belief, it is *okay* for unromantics to express their feelings . . .
. . . feelings of joy . . . when we catch a big one.
. . . feelings of affection . . . for our favorite putter.
. . . feelings of fear . . . when our mother-in-law comes to visit.
. . . feelings of resentment . . . when Valentine's Day rolls around.
. . . feelings of love . . . for our favorite quarterback.

783

"By all means marry. If you get a good wife, you will become happy; if you get a bad one, you will become a philosopher."
~ Socrates

❧ SEX, SEX, SEX, SEX, SEX, SEX, SEX, SEX, SEX AND MORE SEX ❧

784-786

While macho men *never* cry, unromantic men sometimes *do* cry... under these circumstances:

- When our cable TV company raises its prices.
- When our team loses the Superbowl.
- When our mother-in-law comes to visit.
- When we receive the charge card bill from our wives' shopping sprees.

787

- Most romantic TV talk show host (male): Phil Donahue
- *Least* romantic TV talk show host (male): Rush Limbaugh
- Most romantic TV talk show host (female): Oprah Winfrey
- *Least* romantic TV talk show host (female): Joan Rivers

788

"You never really know a man until you have divorced him."
~ Zsa Zsa Gabor

Sex, Sex, Sex

789

If she's made you sit through sappy movies like *Love* Story, *Ghost* and *On Golden Pond*, then I'd say *you* have a right to make her sit through *The Notorious Daughter of Fanny Hill*, *Massage Parlor Wife* and *The Lustful Turk*. These films, and hundreds more, are now available on video. For those who follow such things, these are among a genre of films called "sexploitation" movies—most are from the 60s, but they range from the 40s through the early 70s. A catalog of these unusual offerings is available for just 3 bucks from S.W.V. Catalog, Dept. F.U.N., P.O. Box 33664, Seattle, WA 98155.

✦ SEX! ✦

790

"Sex is God's joke on human beings."
~ Bette Davis

791

For your Unromantic Reading List:

Anything by Dr. Ruth. It's not that the information isn't accurate or helpful . . . it's just that I can't take the pint-sized, German-accented doctor *seriously*. (And I think I finally figured-out why she is so obsessed with talking about *penises*: Dr. Ruth's face is eye-level with the average man's crotch!)

792

Just to prove to you that I don't need to *make-up* stuff in order to be unromantic and outrageous . . . here's an unedited quote from a full-page ad in one of the major men's magazines:

"EUROPE'S SEXUAL BREAKTHROUGH THAT'S NOW LEGAL HERE! Yes! A totally invisible super stimulant that makes women crave hot, wild sex after just 60 seconds exposure! It's medical science's ultimate 'Weapon of Pleasure'! Imagine! A perfectly legal sexual stimulant cleverly masked in a man's cologne that when unknowingly inhaled by any adult woman: Unblocks all restraints, all resistance—fires up the raw, animal sex-drive in every woman's body—burns her into your willing and eager 'sexual slave' for up to 8 straight hours at a time! . . . A sexual bombshell has just been exploded by European doctors that has turned the bedrooms of France, England, Germany and Italy into nightly marathons of wild, reckless pleasure."

You get the picture. The ad goes on like this for quite a while, and finally offers you *Submit*—the "Foreplay In a Bottle" cologne—for only $29.95. [Y'know, I must be in the wrong business. Why am I writing books when I could be making a killing in toll-free sex lines and guaranteed aphrodisiacs?!?] Anyway, if you have an excess of money or a shortage of intelligence, send your $29.95 to Image Tec Co., 163 Denton Ave., Lynbrook, NY 11563.

❥ *HOT STUFF!* ❥

793

It may not be romantic, but a "Lollipop Condom" will certainly get your guy's attention! They come in red, yellow and blue—and they're wrapped in clear plastic... just like a real lollipop. 3 for $6.98! From the *Funny Side Up* catalog: Call 215-361-5130; or write 425 Stump Rd., P.O. Box 2800, North Wales, PA 19454.

794

Make *her* sleep in the wet spot.

795

Guys, if you really want to cut through the romantic bullshit and just get a girl into bed with you, I recommend that you read *Cosmopolitan* magazine. *Really!* Here are a few article titles from some recent issues:

"Women Who Say Yes to Sex but No to Love"
"No More Nice Girls"
"How to Hold a Man By Giving Him His Freedom"
"How to Have Sex Anywhere"
"A Slut from East Toledo"
"Boobs, Boys and High Heels"

Sports, Sports, Sports

796

All sports are unromantic . . . but these are the most unromantic, ranked in order:

> Hunting
> Fishing
> Boxing
> Rugby
> Hockey
> Football
> Lacrosse
> Wrestling

You see, the more *violent* a sport is, the more unromantic—and truly *manly*—it is. Hunting and fishing, which involve outright *killing*, are the most unromantic of all, because they approach the *ultimate sport of all*, which is War. Think about it.

797

How could you even *think* of going to Paris on holiday when you haven't yet visited the recently-opened Hockey Hall of Fame in Toronto?! The new facility includes a copy of the Montreal Canadiens' dressing room, plus a re-creation of a 1950s living room, complete with a black-and-white TV set showing "Hockey Night in Canada." I'm not much of a hockey fan myself, but I'm flushed with excitement just *thinking* about it. The museum is located at 30 Yonge St. in downtown Toronto. Call 'em at 416-360-7765.

798

Personally, when it comes to hockey, I'm partial to the Boston Bruins. But my first love is basketball—especially the Boston Celtics. And, wouldn't you know it, the famous statues of both Larry Bird and Bobby Orr are housed in the Sports Museum of New England... *another* great unromantic vacation destination. Let your spouse walk the Freedom Trail and visit Paul Revere's house, while you peruse the memorabilia, videos and displays on the Red Sox, Celtics, Bruins—and even the hapless Patriots. Plan a trip to East Cambridge—call 'em at 617-57-SPORT.

799

Golf is the ultimate, perfect dodge.

○ It takes a lot of time to play a round—so it keeps you out of the house.
○ You get to ride around in a little go-cart. You get to wear goofy clothes.
○ You get to buy new toys and accessories endlessly.
○ You get to subscribe to all kinds of fun magazines and newsletters.
○ You can turn most business meetings into a round of golf. m You can turn *every* vacation into a week of golf.
○ You can talk in golf jargon, which few women understand. m It's expensive—leaving little money left over for romantic foolishness.
○ You can justify the expense and the time by saying it will help your career!

800

When the typical unromantic speaks of "sports" it almost always refers to *spectator* sports. We may be unromantic, but many of us don't particularly like to break a sweat. However—there is a sizable group of unromantics who utilize *participation* sports as a way to avoid being romantic. I tip my hat to them. This is further proof that you can twist anything—from couch-potato TV watching to marathon-running—into an unromantic activity.

❥ SURPRISE! ❥

801

* Pitchers—romantic
* Catchers—unromantic
* First basemen—unromantic
* Second basemen—romantic
* Third basemen—insecure, but romantic
* Shortstops—nervous, twitchy fellows (unromantic)
* Left fielders—unromantic
* Right fielders—romantic
* Center fielders—romantic on alternate days

802

"I would rather score a touchdown than make love to the prettiest girl in the United States."
~ Paul Hornung

Surprise!

803

Questionable Romantic Role Model:
Leo Buscaglia

Author of *Love; Born For Love; Living, Loving & Learning; Personhood; Loving Each Other;* and well-known and well-loved for his heart-warming lectures on PBS.

P.S.—Leo is in his 60s, he's single and never been married. Does he know something he's not telling us?!?

142 ◆ 1001 WAYS **NOT** TO BE ROMANTIC

❧ SURPRISE! ❧

804

Unromantics have their artistic side, too, you know. But we have definite tastes. Here's an artistic primer for you beginners:

- ❖ Unromantics prefer Cubism to Impressionism
- ❖ Unromantics prefer Modernism to Romanticism (obviously).
- ❖ Unromantics prefer abstract art to realistic art.
- ❖ Unromantics prefer Giacometti to Michelangelo.

Reprinted with permission of United Feature Syndicate, Inc., Rose Is Rose © 1993

805

One surprising finding was that bureaucrats and employees of the Department of Motor Vehicles *are* romantic! My researchers were originally convinced that the incompetence and vacant looks on the faces of bureaucrats was evidence of dedicated *un*romantics. But the exact *opposite* is true! It turns out that instead of doing their jobs, these people are daydreaming and scheming romantic plans that they spring on their lovers every single night! Go figure!

806

Here's a surprise: Truck drivers *are* romantic! Here's why: 1) "Absence makes the heart grow fonder," and 2) They spend hours on the road listening to country western songs on the radio.

807

Anyone who looks like or sounds like H. Ross Perot is an honorary unromantic, regardless of other factors.

The Beer Barrel Polka

808

Yo! Listen up! I just discovered Beer Across America—a "beer-of-the-month club"! For just $14.94 per month, they'll mail you two six-packs, each from a different small brewer. *Yow!* Call 800-854-2337.

809

Another reason to visit Denver: More beer is brewed in Metropolitan Denver than anywhere else in the United States. And mark your calendar for the second week in October, when Denver hosts the Great American Beer Festival!

810

"Marriage is based on the theory that when a man discovers a brand of beer exactly to his taste he should at once throw up his job and go to work in the brewery."
~ George Jean Nathan

811

For the fanatical beer lover: *Beer Labels of the World*, by Bill Yenne. Yes, just what you've been yearning for: A big, hardcover book with photos of *thousands* of beer labels! Includes some of the rarest and most unique labels from around the globe.

◆ THE FAR SIDE ◆

812

Be on the lookout for... Dixie White Moose beer—a white chocolate beer! [I don't know whether to be excited or disgusted!] From Dixie Brewing Co. of New Orleans. Also... Watch for Birra Perfetto beer—made from oregano and other Italian spices! From Pike Place Brewery of Seattle. And while you're at it... Pete's Wicked Ale—one of the country's fastest-growing brands, includes raspberries in its recipe! From Pete's Brewing Co. of Palo Alto, California.

813-818

Least romantic types of music:
- Polkas
- Dixieland
- Anything by Madonna
- Irish drinking songs
- Rap
- Russian rock 'n roll

The Far Side

819

Traveling by bus has to be the single most unromantic method of transportation yet devised by man. A nice comfy Greyhound bus; traveling across America's scenic superhighways; stopping at exotic McDonald's Restaurants—what a way to create some truly special memories with your lover!

♠ *SURPRISE!* ♠

820-822

- ♠ Pick-up trucks with gun racks.
- ♠ Any car or truck with over-sized tires.
- ♠ Any car or truck with a booming stereo that registers 6.2 on the Richter Scale.

823

Where *not* to meet members of the opposite sex: Health clubs. First, let's clarify one thing—"Health clubs" is just a Yuppie way of saying "gym." You know—sweaty, smelly gyms. Now, remember that most of us are not at our best in the gym. We're out of shape. The guys are wearing sweaty T-shirts and ragged shorts. The gals are wearing Spandex outfits that accentuate every ounce of flab. We're all flexing and grimacing and grunting. Is this a good way to meet members of the opposite sex?? I think not.

824-825

If she's tired of *Cosmo*, and you're looking for something more "interesting" than *Penthouse* . . . you may want to investigate these two European magazines you won't find at the corner newsstand:

<<O>> *Fashion and Fantasies*—"Direct from Germany, this slick magazine covers the latest leather, rubber and PVC fashions. Color photographs illustrate the latest fashions from the main European designers in fantasy styles. Coffee table quality. Text in English." Just $29.

Skin Two—"England's high quality, fantasy fashion magazine. You'll be delighted by the *Skin Two* collection of leather, rubber and PVC outfits. Plus wickedly high heels and seamed stockings. Photography by Trevor Watson and Grace Lau. check out our special *World Bulletin* reviewing the hottest events, shops and more!" Only $25.

Available from Intimate Treasures, P.O. Box 77902, Dept. 1CS100193, San Francisco, CA 94107; or call 415-896-0944.

826-827

More unromantic vacations:

✓ If you liked *Jurassic Park*, you'll *love* the "Digging Dinosaurs" project in the Hell Creek badlands of Makoshika State Mark in Glendive, Montana. For only $875 you get to be a volunteer and crawl around and dig in the dirt. Wow! Call 406-994-3170.

✓ Take an "Adventure Eco-Cruise" to Antarctica! I don't know about you, but Antarctica is high on my list—well above Hawaii, Paris, Australia or Tahiti! And the price! —A steal at only $4,995 per person! Call quick! —Mountain Travel/Sobek, at 800-227-2384.

828

"Every man plays the fool once in his life, but to marry is playing the fool all one's life long."
~ William Congreve

The Gospel According to Joe

829

Romance is a state of mind. It's called "insanity."

830

Most of life isn't romantic *anyway*—it's filled with things like taking out the garbage, watching TV and other distractions like going to work. But you can make **anything** unromantic if you'll only try.

✦ THE GOSPEL ACCORDING TO JOE ✦

831

It is the *natural state* of humankind to be unromantic. How many people do you know who have great, romantic relationships? One, maybe *two*, out of the thousands of people you know. If we were *supposed* to be romantic, it would unfold *naturally*. Nobody has to teach a rose how to grow and bloom—*right*?! I say we should stop trying to achieve some kind of romantic utopia that the poets write about. I say leave romance to the poets, and let the rest of us get on with our lives!

832

Unromantics are fiercely independent, but not especially philosophical. Our philosophy, such as it is, may be summed-up in these simple statements: "Stay outta my face!" and "Who the hell are *you* to tell *me* what to do?!"

"WE HAVE TO TALK? SURE, GIVE ME A CALL AT HALFTIME."

833

Just as there is a skinny person inside of every fat person, I believe there is an unromantic person inside every romantic. I believe that every "sensitive male" longs to act like a chauvinist pig, whistle at girls in short skirts, and generally act like a college sophomore. I believe that every sweet and romantic woman longs to tell most men where to shove it; to slouch around in comfortable, baggy, out-of-style clothes; and to have a quick, passionate, meaningless affair with a stranger.

834

Unromantics are proudly, arrogantly, romantically and politically *incorrect!*

The Heartbreak of VD

835-839

- Valentine's Day is penance for the rest of the year.
- Valentine's Day is the Holiday from Hell.
- Valentine's Day is about *obligation*—not about love.
- Valentine's Day is proof that God is a woman.
- Valentine's Day was created by a secret pact among FTD, Fanny Farmer, Hallmark and the Devil.

840

For Valentine's Day, buy her lingerie that's two sizes too small. (It will motivate her to lose weight. She'll appreciate the gesture. Trust me.)

841

Most creative excuse for having forgotten Valentine's Day: "No, honey, I didn't forget Valentine's Day! —It's just that you're too special to be celebrated on the same day as everybody else!"

842

It is somehow appropriate that Valentine's Day is stuck in the dead of winter, isn't it?!

The Way We Were

843

Let's just take a moment to think back to that great, great year 1966 . . . when miniskirts became the rage. —Nothing since then has even come close to being so wonderful.

844

If you want to take a truly unromantic vacation, visit the restored Mormon village of Nauvoo, Illinois. Referred to as the "Williamsburg of the Midwest," this town is described as "a four-day experience." There are tours of 25 authentically restored shops and homes that are reminiscent of the mid-1880s. One of the highlights of the tours is the gravesite of Joseph Smith, founder of the Church of Jesus Christ of Latter-day Saints. For more information, call the Western Illinois Tourism Council at 800-232-3889.

845

Another truly unromantic vacation is a visit to the American Clock and Watch Museum. Located in beautiful downtown Bristol, Connecticut, the museum boasts 1,700 clocks, 1,600 watches, and tens of thousands of books, catalogs, photographs and documents. (Be still, my heart!) Please mark your calendar: The museum is only open March through November! For more information, call 203-583-6070.

❖ BUT THEN—WHO CARES WHAT JOE THINKS?! ❖

The World According to Joe

846

If we unromantics seem a bit *defensive*, it's because we're persecuted and discriminated against in this Politically Correct, Post-Feminist period of American life. Just try to talk about it on *Donahue* or *Oprah*! If *they* don't manipulate you and embarrass you, the *audience* will! (We should start a Society for the Prevention of Discrimination Against the Uncurably Unromantic!)

847-856

Joe's Top 10 Reasons for Getting Married

1. To have someone to scratch that spot in the middle of my back that I just can't reach.
2. To have someone to put my cold feet on in the middle of the night.
3. A great tax deduction.
4. Sex, sex, sex!
5. I can't cook to save my life!
6. To get my mother to stop bugging me.
7. My friends are starting to think I'm gay.
8. The house could use a good cleaning.
9. To get out of debt.
10. Oh, *why not*?!

857-860

The least romantic seasons:

Spring: Rain, mud, spring cleaning, taxes due
Summer: Hot, humid, kids home from school, mosquitoes
Autumn: Back-to-school, Back-to-work
Winter: Cold, snow, shoveling the driveway, Christmas shopping

❧ *TRAVEL TIPS* ❧

861

The reason I am so confident that the unromantic lifestyle will prevail is that **romance has no survival value!** You see, humans are the *only* species out of the millions of species on the planet that exhibits the curious behavior of romance. Romance has proven to be of no interest or value to the vast majority of life on earth. If we don't kill ourselves off with our passionate/romantic/emotional natures, then what *will* happen is that the romantics will slowly die-off. This is because the romantics are more interested in "love" than in sex. Thus, they breed less often, producing fewer romantic offspring.

862-872

Let's clarify . . .

Romantic	Unromantic
Jay Leno	David Letterman
Wine	Beer
Saturday	Monday
Glenn Miller	Rap
Corvettes	Chevy Novas
Filet mignon	Pizza
Cosby	Roseanne
Poconos	Pittsburgh
Bridges of Madison County	*Bridges of Newark, New Jersey*
The Ritz	The No-Tell Motel

Travel Tips

873

More reasons to *just stay home:* The Colorado Desert is in California. Virginia City is in Nevada. Michigan City is in Indiana. The Florida Mountains are in New Mexico. Kansas City is in Missouri. And the Wyoming Valley is in Pennsylvania.

✦ TRAVEL TIPS ✦

874-877

While visiting Los Angeles (a *glamorous*, if not exactly *romantic* city), you may want to visit these truly unromantic museums:

○ **Forrest Ackerman's Sci-Fi & Monster Mansion** : This accumulation of more than 300,000 items is the largest collection of horror/sci-fi/fantasy memorabilia in the world! Included is the original robot from *Metropolis*, models for *King Kong*, and miniatures from *Star Wars*, *Close Encounters* and *Gremlins*. By appointment, call 213-MOON-FAN.

○ **Frederick's of Hollywood Lingerie Museum** : You might think this would be romantic, but these items are for movie buffs, curiosity-seekers and other kinky people—but not for romantics: Madonna's bustier; a (32B) bra signed by Cher; and Marilyn Monroe's bra from *Let's Make Love*. Visit Frederick's at 6608 Hollywood Blvd., Hollywood, 213-466-5151.

○ **The Doorknob Museum**: You'll thrill to not only antique doorknobs, but to elegant pulls, push-plates and doorstops! The owner of the museum is a bona fide member of the Antique Doorknob Collectors of America, lest you doubt his sincerity. By appointment only! 1228 W. Manchester Ave., 213-759-0344.

○ **The Air Conditioning & Refrigeration Industry Museum** : This unique museum won't leave you cold! [Get it?!] Featured are things that beat the heat . . . old Coca-Cola coolers and iceboxes, ice crushers, ice hooks and all kinds of ice makers! Wow! By appointment only! 2220 S. Hill St., 213-747-0291.

○ **Long Beach Firefighters Museum** : [Make-up your *own* pun here.] If you're into old pumpers and ladder wagons, visit these dedicated firefighters at 1445 Peterson Ave., Long Beach, 310-597-0351.

878

Shopping Strategy #202: Buy that special "I love you gift" at the airport giftshop on your way home.

879

Travel Trivia: The Greater Detroit area has the highest concentration of doughnut shops in America.

880

If you can't afford a *stripper* to entertain at your partner's birthday party, but you *still* want to do something tasteless, here's the answer! The *Happy Birthday Strip Tease Video*. Yes, there's a male version and a female version. Only $11.98! From the *Funny Side Up* catalog: Call 215-361-5130; or write 425 Stump Rd., P.O. Box 2800, North Wales, PA 19454.

Truly Tasteless

881

A truly unromantic yet tasteless book: *Love Love and Love*, by Sandra Bernhard. I quote from *Publishers Weekly*: "This odd, haphazard collection of self-indulgent 'essays' (some just half a page long) and poems tries to depict the frustration of relationships in the '90s—sexual, yet barren and unfulfilling. Before long, through repetition and banality, the pieces focus mainly on sex—not love—and become odes to fellatio, cunnilingus and innumerable scatological poses." The author's qualifications for being a writer? —She appears on *Roseanne* and she has posed nude for *Playboy*.

882

When I think of unromantic places to visit, Vietnam and Laos top *my* list. Some of you may be excited to hear that Laos recently relaxed its tourism restrictions, and now allows 5,000 visitors a year—up from 4,200 in 1992. (True!) I think you'd better hurry so you can avoid the crowds! Quick! Call Wings of the World at 800-465-8687, or Absolute Asia at 800-736-8187.

883

Crotchless panties.

884

Chocolates shaped like penises and breasts. Send for a catalog! Private Parts Adult Chocolates, 355 W. Main St., Suite 119, Norristown, PA 19401.

Unromantic Classics

885

An Unromantic Classic: Forget her birthday.

886

An Unromantic Classic: Forget your anniversary.

887

An Unromantic Classic: Morning breath.

888

An Unromantic Classic: Call her by your previous girlfriend's name. You get Bonus Points for doing it more than once in a single evening. {Thanks to G.C.}

889-891

Books for your Unromantics Library:

- ♠ *Love Is Hell*, by Matt Groening (creator of The Simpsons). *Love Is Hell* is *funny* as hell!
- ♠ *A Marriage Made In Heaven—or—Too Tired for an Affair*, by Erma Bombeck. I think the title says it all.
- ♠ *Is Sex Necessary?* by James Thurber & E.B. White. This classic from earlier this century is still relevant, insightful, and hilarious!

Unromantic Ideas

892-894

- ☞ Become a workaholic.
- ☞ Become a writer.
- ☞ Become a husband.

895

Unromantic accessory #3: *Mirrored sunglasses*. If she can't see your eyes, she can't tell if you're looking intently at her, ogling some other women, or dozing.

896

Unromantic pastime #82: *Bicycle riding*. Even though watching girls in shorts ride bicycles is perhaps one of the most wonderful sights on earth, it still can't overcome the downside of bicycle-riding for men—which is that any bicycle excursion of more than 200 yards makes your groin go numb.

✦ VIRTUAL REALITY ✦

897

Unromantic vacation idea #204: If simplicity and elegance are the heart of romance, then Las Vegas must be the capital for unromantics like us. First, there's the greatest rip-off in the world, gambling. Second, there's Wayne Newton. Third, there's all those gaudy hotels. Fourth, there's the annual Elvis Performers Showcase. Call your travel agent *now*!

898

Become a laserdisc fanatic. It will chew up your vacation fund, your life savings and your retirement fund in nothing flat. {Thanks to C.S.}

Virtual Reality

899

The most unromantic day of the year? April 15th.

900

Another truly pointless place to visit is the Route 66 Hall of Fame. (Remember "I get my kicks/On Route 66"?) Located at a truck stop in McLean, Illinois, the hall is a shrine dedicated "to average folks and the state's portion of the 2,400-mile highway." Wow! Those Illinoisers really know how to create an attraction, don't they? Perhaps they should be consulting with the uncreative people at Disney World. (They run a little theme park in Orlando, Florida.)

901

Cartoons have come a *long* way since Bugs Bunny. The Excalibur Films collection makes *Cool World* look stone cold! You can get a full color catalog listing hundreds of erotic cartoons available on video. The catalog is just $3, from Intimate Treasures, P.O. Box 77902, Dept. 1CS100193, San Francisco, CA 94107; or call 415-896-0944.

902

Future unromantics will be able to take advantage of "virtual sex" (that's "sex without the knotty complications of sustained conversation, communicable diseases or brunch" according to the *New York Times*—really!) and "virtual relationships" (wherein you can create your mate to your very own personal specifications!)

903

But for those of us stuck in the tail end of the 20th Century, the closest we can come to "virtual sex" is to fantasize about it with the help of *Future Sex* magazine. Described as "Cyberporn," the magazine is dedicated to the proposition that "Computer science is changing the way we think about sex," according to editor Lisa Palac.

904

Because of the thinner air, a golf ball travels about 10 percent farther at Lake Tahoe's 6,200-foot elevation than at sea level.

Wedding Bell Blues

905

Item to be filed under "Tackiest Weddings": It seems that every year, the *Live With Regis & Kathie Lee* TV show holds a contest in which couples write in, explaining why they should be chosen to be wed on the show on Valentine's Day.

906

Unromantics cross their fingers while reciting their wedding vows.

907

A sure way to drain the romance out of your engagement is to plan your wedding *together*. There was a *good reason* for the tradition of having the bride and her mother plan the wedding, and keeping the groom out of it. Look at it this way: If you were going to host an elegant party for the 100 people you care most about, would you hire an hysterical woman and a know-nothing man to plan the affair for you?

908

The Most Unromantic Wedding of All Time: Took place in Madison Square Garden in 1982, when 4,000 Moonies got married in a mass wedding ceremony.

Weird & Wacky

909-920

Items from the Unromantics Hall of Fame

- The first TV remote control unit.
- The complete collection of "Mr. Bill" film clips from *Saturday Night Live*.
- The first twist-off beer bottle cap.
- A selection of various power tools.
- Cars. Lots of cars. All makes, all sizes. All in need of repair.
- A pair of unwashed socks worn by Larry Bird in his last NBA Playoff game.
- Some big stogies: One from David Letterman; one from Art Buchwald; one from Bill Cosby.
- A chastity belt.
- A garter belt worn by Madonna.
- The collar worn by Spuds MacKenzie.
- The collar worn by Madonna during her 1989 "Sluts Around the World" Tour.
- My awesome beer can collection from college.

♦ WEIRD & WACKY ♦

921

For the *ultimate* in unromantic gifts, do your shopping at the Los Angeles County Coroner's Office. Yes! They now offer a "Skeletons in the Closet" line of gifts! The most popular items include toe tags, body bags, T-shirts and beach towels imprinted with chalk body outlines, and assorted coffee mugs and tote bags—among other post-mortem paraphernalia. Give 'em a call, and do your Christmas and Valentine's shopping early! Call 213-343-0512.

922

For your Unromantic Reading List:
Everything by Stephen King. *Aaaaaaiiiiiiiieeeeeeeeeee!*

923

Forget the candy and roses . . . If you *really* want to surprise your partner, come home from work wearing a "Conehead" domed head mask. It won't do much for your love life—but you'll look so stupid that your partner will probably forget why she's mad at you for a while. Only $14.98. From the *Funny Side Up* catalog: Call 215-361-5130; or write 425 Stump Rd., P.O. Box 2800, North Wales, PA 19454.

924

The perfect gift for the accountant, engineer or all-around nerd in your life: The "Nerd Crossing" street sign. This 18-inch square galvanized steel reproduction conforms to U.S. Highway specifications for years of outdoor or indoor use. Only $35 from—who else—those fun-loving folks at MIT. Write or call the MIT Museum Shop: 617-253-4462, or 265 Massachusetts Ave., Cambridge, MA 03139.

➧ WHO CARES?!? ➧

What Do Women Want?

925

"The great question that has never been answered and which I have not yet been able to answer, despite my thirty years of research into the feminine soul, is: What does woman want?"
~ Sigmund Freud

926

"None of your business."
~ Ursula K. Le Guin

What's Your Sign?

927-938

Which sign of the Zodiac is the *most* romantic? *Least* romantic? You decide!

Aries [March 20-April 20]
Aries people are . . . generous, great leaders . . . and selfish, thoughtless, aggressive, impulsive and have little regard for the consequences of their actions, rash, unable to finish what they start.

Taurus [April 20-May 20]
Taurus people are . . . stable, organized . . . and obstinate, blindly prejudiced, materialistic, and possessive of objects.

Gemini [May 21-June 21]
Gemini people are . . . intelligent, versatile . . . and restless, shallow, unreliable, self-deceptive, and prone to double-talk.

Cancer [June 21-July 22]
Cancer people are . . . imaginative, caring . . . and stingy, irritable, melancholy, clingy, cowardly, moody, possessive, and secretive.

Leo [July 22-August 23]
Leo people are . . . leaders, daring . . . and arrogant, vane, tyrannical, haughty, romantically promiscuous, and have to be in charge regardless of whether they're qualified or not.

Virgo [August 23-September 23]
Virgo people are . . . clear thinkers, cool-headed . . . and cranky, pessimistic, timid, picky, and critical.

Libra [September 23-October 23]
Libra people are . . . fair-minded, good arbitrators . . . and lazy, indecisive, argumentative, selfishly pleasure-seeking, and prone to procrastination.

♦ WHEEL OF FORTUNE ♦

Scorpio [October 23-November 22]
Scorpio people are... sharp, insightful... and ruthless, fanatical, vengeful, sadistic, suspicious, self-loathing, and resentful of anyone questioning them.

Sagittarius [November 22-December 21]
Sagittarius people are... optimistic, risk-takers... and reckless, careless, rude, fickle, confused, lack tact, and are brutally honest.

Capricorn [December 21-January 20]
Capricorn people are... practical, good counselors... and selfish, narrow-minded, ruthlessly ambitious, rigid, snobby, lonely, and depressed.

Aquarius [January 20-February 19]
Aquarius people are... curious, gregarious... and neurotic, eccentric, detached, absentminded, uncooperative, they run late, and they childishly insist on things being their way.

Pisces [February 19-March 20]
Pisces people are... creative, dreamers... and timid, masochistic, apprehensive, good liars, weak willed, and irresponsible with money.

Wheel of Fortune

939

They say that jewelry is romantic. *Not so*, according to R. Snodgrass, of St. Louis. Says he bought his wife a long gold chain. She wore it to bed, rolled over and strangled herself to death.

940

Have you ever wondered what Americans would do if they didn't have television? Well, here's a hint from recent history: In 1965 there was a massive power blackout—for just one night—in the northeastern U.S.; the birth rate rose significantly nine months later.

941

Tattoos are rather unromantic. The most unromantic of all are tattoos that include your girlfriend's name. All of your future girlfriends—not to mention wives—will be royally pissed-off. One Hell's Angel I know took to only dating girls named Heather. A sad, sad story.

942

Pinball. Video games. Arcade games.

Where's the Beef?

943

You can't be a "Sensitive Guy" and an unromantic at the same time. You've got to make up your mind—choose your side. Some "Sensitive Guy" role models include Alan Alda, Phil Donahue, Gregory J.P. Godek, Robert Bly, John Bradshaw and Bill Clinton.

944

The most unromantic magazines:

- ▼ *Ms. Magazine*: No sense of humor here!
- ▼ *Mad Magazine*: All sense of humor here!
- ▼ *New Republic*: Who do these blow-hards think they are?!
- ▼ *Field and Stream*: Ah—Now *there's* a magazine!
- ▼ *Hustler*
- ▼ *The New England Journal of Medicine*

945

Are you old enough to remember when the phrase "Going to the submarine races," was a code for going parking? But in Fort Lauderdale, Florida, the races are the real thing! The International Submarine Races take place in mid-June. For more info call 800-22-SUNNY, extension 711.

946

Ogle other women in public.

Where's Waldo?

947

Romantic or unromantic?—*You* decide: The *Dark Shadows* Fan Club. (P.O. Box 92, Maplewood, NJ 07040.)

948

How appropriate that the least romantic site in the entire continental United States is *also* in one of the least romantic states. South Dakota is home to Custer State Park, which is the site of . . . Mount Rushmore! What could be more inspiring than the 60-foot-high sculptures of those great romantics George Washington, Thomas Jefferson, Abraham Lincoln and Theodore Roosevelt! Ah—many a fair maiden has fallen into a swoon 'neath the imposing, masculine figures, as her beau recited the Gettysburg Address or Inaugural Speech of Theodore Roosevelt. Ah, love!

949

Unromantics are bed hogs and cover-stealers.

950

More unromantic role models:
- Barney Fyfe
- Barney Rubble
- Barney

Who Asked *You*?

951

"But isn't there a time and a place for romance?" You might ask? Well, yes there is. *One* is when you're 18 years old and you don't know any better. *Another* is when it's the only way you can think of to have sex with her.

952

"The only really happy folk are married women and single men."
~ H.L. Mencken

953

Unromantic organizations:
- **MENSA:** These people are too smart for their own good!
- **NRA:** "Happiness is a warm gun"?!
- **Shriners:** It's categorically impossible to be romantic while wearing a fez.
- **The Unification Church**: If you like hanging-out at airports.
- **The American Bar Association**: Lawyers unite!
- **Laboratory Animal Management Association**: "If you like rats, join us!"
- **Baker Street Irregulars**: The Sherlock Holmes Society.

954

"Love is the wisdom of the fool and the folly of the wise."
~ Samuel Johnson

Why Bother?

955-966

Twelve months of unromantic events to celebrate:

January—is National Prune Breakfast Month. The 28th is National Kazoo Day.

February—is National Snack Food Month. The 19th is Temporary Insanity Day.

March—is National Welding Month. It's also National Peanut Month. The 22nd is National Goof-Off Day.

April—is National Anxiety Month. Taxes are due April 15th.

May—is Better Sleep Month. It's also National Barbecue Month.

June—is National Adopt-A-Cat Month. The 24th is Flying Saucer Day.

July—is National Baked Bean Month. The 28th is Hamburger Day.

August—is National Parks Month. The 13th is International Left-Handers Day.

September— is National Piano Month. The 22nd is Hobbit Day.

October—is National Adopt-A-Dog Month.

November—is National Stamp Collecting Month. It's also International Drum Month. The 6th is Saxophone Day.

December—is Made In America Month. The 12th is National Ding-A-Ling Day. The 26th is National Whiner's Day.

Wilted Flowers

967

Unromantics go into hibernation from February 1st though the 15th. They then poke their heads up, and if they see their wife's shadow looming over them, they scurry back into hiding, and sleep for another six weeks (until the Valentine's Season is well behind them).

968

Item to be filed under "Couldn't we do something better with all this money?" FTD reports that more than 35 million roses were delivered last Valentine's Day. Let's see... at an average price of $50 a dozen, that comes to... $145,833,333! A nice bit of change, eh?!

969

It would be very unromantic to get your wife a customized license plate with her initials if here name were...

Helen Ann Garrity
Pamela Michelle Smith
Jenny Elizabeth White
Tracy Isabelle Tate
Zelda Ida Tobin
Cynthia Olivia Wagner
Patricia Ida Gardener

970

Seemingly romantic questions that invariably lead to arguments:
- "*Why* do you love me?"
- "What do you like *best* about me?"
- "How could we improve our sex life?"

✦ WOMEN'S LIB ✦

971

And still *more* unromantic role models (for boys):

- ✓ Sam Kinneson
- ✓ Albert Einstein
- ✓ Barry Goldwater
- ✓ Andy Rooney
- ✓ Pope John Paul II
- ✓ Max Headroom

972

And some unromantic role models (for girls):

- ✖ Murphy Brown
- ✖ Bella Abzug
- ✖ Phyllis Shafley
- ✖ Edith Bunker
- ✖ Aunt Bea

Women's Lib

973

"I'm furious at the Women's Liberationists. They keep getting up on soapboxes and proclaiming that women are brighter than men. That's true, but it should be kept very quiet or it ruins the whole racket."
~ Anita Loos

974

"A woman who strives to be like a man lacks ambition."
~ Anonymous

✦ X-RATED ✦

975

Thank you, Betty Friedan. The Women's Liberation Movement is perhaps the single greatest advancement in the unromantics' cause in the 20th Century. Prior to the 1960s, our culture's gender roles and stable beliefs required at least a *minimal* level of courtesy and romance in our relationships. But since the advent of Women's Lip [oops—"Lib"], courtesy is passé, and romance is sexist.

976

"No one is going to take Women's Liberation seriously until women recognize that they will not be thought of as equals in the secret privacy of men's most private mental parts until they eschew alimony."
~ Norman Mailer

X-Rated

977

X-Rated fortune cookies. Need I say more? A dozen Chinese fortune cookies for just $2.98! From the *Funny Side Up* catalog: Call 215-361-5130; or write 425 Stump Rd., P.O. Box 2800, North Wales, PA 19454.

978

I tried satin sheets once. She was impressed. I slid off the slippery satin sheets during foreplay and broke my ankle. Verdict: *Not* romantic.

979

Copenhagen now has an Erotic Museum, founded by Ole Ege, a Danish photographer of nudes. The museum is spread over four floors, with the exhibits getting more risqué the higher up you go!

✦ 1-800-OOH-LA-LA ✦

980

Sexual Positions: A Sensual Guide to Lovemaking. The book...and now—the *video*! Sexy?—Yes. Educational?—Yes. Romantic?—No! Why?? Well, the book is so graphic...and the video is so...um...graphic and sexy and wow, you should see the bodies on those girls, with their heaving—well, ahem—anyway...The video is so good that, well, most guys feel no need for a real woman! The book is only $14.95, and the video is just $24.95, from the *Playboy Catalog*. Call 800-423-9494; or write *Playboy Catalog*, P.O. Box 809, Itasca, IL 60143.

981

The Clitoral Kiss, by Kenneth Ray Stubbs, Ph.D. Frankly, I'm not sure if this book is romantic or *not* . . . but the title surely is intriguing! If you're too embarrassed to ask for it at your local bookstore—*I* was—contact the publisher, Secret Garden Press, P.O. Box 67-KCA, Larkspur, CA 94977.

982

"It is naive in the extreme for women to expect to be regarded as equals by men . . . so long as they persist in a subhuman (i.e., animal-like) behavior during sexual intercourse. I'm referring . . . to the outlandish PANTING, GASPING, MOANING, SOBBING, WRITHING, SCRATCHING, BITING, SCREAMING conniptions, and the seemingly invariable 'OH MY GOD . . . OH MY GOD . . . OH MY GOD' all so predictably integral to pre-, post-, and orgasmic stages of intercourse."
~ Terry Southern

983

"Men have been trained and conditioned by women, not unlike the way Pavlov conditioned his dogs, into becoming their slaves. As compensation for their labors men are given periodic use of women's vaginas."
~ Esther Vilar

1001 WAYS *NOT* TO BE ROMANTIC ✦ 171

♦ YOUR PROFESSION... ♦

Your Profession: Romantic or Unromantic?

984-995

Astronomers—unromantic
Astrologers—romantic
Accountants—huh?
Bassoonists—romantic
Balloonists—romantic
Barbers—unromantic
Bakers—romantic
Bankers/tellers—unromantic
Bankers/loan officers—unromantic
Bank robbers—romantic
Business executives/staff—romantic
Business executives/middle management—unromantic
Business executives/vice presidents—romantic
Business executives/presidents—unromantic
Business executives/CEOs—romantic
Cellists—unromantic
Carpenters—romantic
Cartoonists—romantic
Caterers—romantic
Clerks/department store—unromantic
Clerks/boutiques—romantic
Clerks/convenience stores—unromantic
Clerks/Motor Vehicle Department—yeah, *right!*
Computer programmers—unromantic
Doctors/Surgeons—unromantic
Doctors/Dentists—unromantic
Doctors/Gynecologists—unromantic
Doctors/Pediatricians—romantic
Doctors/Podiatrists—romantic
Doctors/Eye-Ear-Nose—unromantic

❦ ...ROMANTIC OR UNROMANTIC? ❦

Doctors/Neurologists—unromantic
Doctors/Orthopedists—romantic
Doctors/all others—unromantic
Dancers—romantic
Electricians—unromantic
Elephant trainers—unromantic
Engineers—seriously unromantic
Factory workers (union)—unromantic
Factory workers (non-union)—romantic
Farmers—romantic
Firefighters—romantic
Fathers—unromantic
Gardeners—romantic
Golf pros—unromantic
Graphic designers—unromantic
Handymen—romantic
Hairstylists—romantic
Homemakers—romantic
Illustrators—romantic
Investment counselors—unromantic
Infantrymen—unromantic
Insurance salesmen—are you *kidding?!?*
Journalists—unromantic
Kindergarten teachers—romantic
Kennel workers—romantic
Lawyers—*ha-ha-ha-ha-ha-ha-ha-ha-ha-ha-ha-ha-ha!*
Lumberjacks—romantic!
Librarians—unromantic on the outside—hot stuff on the inside!
Mathematicians—unromantic
Mechanics—romantic
Mothers/with any children under 2 years—unromantic
Mothers/with 4+ children—unromantic
Mothers/otherwise—romantic
Mailmen—*think* they're romantic but they're *not*
Marines—unromantic
Military officers/lieutenants—unromantic
Military officers/captains—romantic
Military officers/generals—romantic
Motivational speakers—romantic
Musicians—unromantic
Ministers/Baptist—unromantic

◆ *YOUR PROFESSION...* ◆

Your Profession: *Romantic or Unromantic?* (Continued)

Ministers/Methodist—romantic
Ministers/Episcopalian—unromantic
Ministers/Unitarian—*very* romantic
Models—you'd think they'd be romantic, but they ain't.
McDonald's worker—clueless
Nurses—romantic
Nudists—unromantic
Opera singers—romantic
Optometrists—romantic
Ophthalmologists—unromantic
Physical therapists—romantic
Postal workers—unromantic
Plumbers—surprisingly romantic
Politicians—seductive, but not romantic
Physicists—unromantic
Policemen—unromantic
Painters/house—unromantic
Pilots—romantic
Psychologists—romantic
Psychiatrists—unromantic
Painters/portrait—romantic
Painters/abstract—no way!
Publishers—about as unromantic & unimaginative as they come
Printers—romantic
Quarry worker—unromantic
Quality control engineers—unromantic
Radio DJs—romantic
Radiologists—unromantic
Ranchers—romantic
Restauranteurs—unromantic

❥ ...ROMANTIC OR UNROMANTIC? ❥

Supermarket clerks—unromantic
Students/high school/girls—romantic
Students/high school/boys—clueless
Students/college—romantic (Except Harvard students)
Students/graduate level—terrified
Students/medical school—suicidal
Students/law school—Somebody stop them!
Sailors—romantic
Stewardesses/domestic—unromantic
Stewardesses/international—romantic
Starship captains—romantic!
Truck drivers—romantic
Taxi drivers—unromantic
Teachers—romantic
Telephone operators—unromantic
UPS deliverymen—creatively romantic!
Underground workers (miners, subway employees)—unromantic
Veterinarians—Romantic
Virgins—romantic
Writers—romantic
Waiters—romantic
Waitresses—unromantic
Xerox salesmen—unromantic
X-Rated movie actors—unromantic
YMCA directors—romantic
Yodelers—romantic
Zookeepers—unromantic
Zipper manufacturers—romantic

Zzzzzzz

996

Actually, one of the main reasons why sports fans are so irritating to their partners is that they *talk incessantly* about their favorite team, their favorite player, the latest statistics, the latest standings, the latest player trades, the latest . . . uh, strategies . . . Zzz . . . the, uh, Greatest Player of . . . *yawn* . . . All Time . . . and, um . . . Zzzzzzzzzzzzzz.

997

"I've been in love with the same woman for 41 years.
If my wife finds out, she'll kill me!"
~ Henny Youngman

998

If she suggests you go stargazing because "It's so-o-o romantic!" you can accommodate her and squelch the romantic impulse *at the same time* by arming yourself with a 12-inch reflective telescope and an armful of star charts. "Honey, look! It's Andromeda Binary star number A214-22a1-b! Wow!" Zzzzzzzzzzzzzzzzzzzzzzzzzzzzzzzzzzzzzzzzzzz.

999

"Some women and men seem to need each other."
~ Gloria Steinem

✦ ZZZ ✦

1000

Why is it pointless to attempt to teach most men to be romantic? An old folk saying provides the answer:

*"Never try to teach a pig how to sing.
It wastes your time and annoys the pig."*

1001

Adding insult to injury: *Watch golf on TV.* Zzzzzzzzzzzzzz.

◆ UNROMANTIC COUPONS ◆

1001 Ways NOT To Be Romantic
Unromantic Coupon

This coupon is good for one romantic dinner out.
(Now stay off my back for the next year!)

To_____

From_____

1001 Ways NOT To Be Romantic
Unromantic Coupon

This is a kinky sex coupon.
Good for one marathon session. *Anything goes.*
Valid wherever prohibited by law.

To_____

From_____